It's All About
HEAVEN

As Pictured in Scripture

Jeanne Metcalf
Copyright©2020

Cëgullah Publishing
International Copyright © 2022
www.cegullahpublishing.ca

All rights reserved

ISBN # Textbook: 978-1-926489-32-2
ISBN # Workbook: 978-1-926489-31-5
ISBN #- eBook: 978-1-926489-55-1

Cover photo ©istock.com

Cover design by Jeanne Metcalf.

COPYRIGHT MATTERS

This book is an original manuscript by the author, protected by international copyright laws of Canada. Therefore, none of this author's work may be reproduced, in part or in whole, or stored in a retrieval system, or transmitted in any form or by any means, electronic, mechanical, photocopied, recorded or otherwise for commercial use without the *prior written* permission of the author. However, it is possible to receive permission to use short quotations for personal use, or use in a group study, or for permission to copy certain passages, or to make portions of the writings available for overhead viewing. Simply, contact the author[1] to request it.

---

[1] To contact author, see *Contact Page in Appendix*

All scripture quotes originate from KJV², public domain. However, the name of God appears as YeHoVaH, not LORD. See appendix for more information.

---

²KJV refers to all humankind as "man". Unless the passage itself refers to a particular male person, apply the message to all humankind, regardless of gender.

DEDICATION

As author's dedicate their books, often, they honour members of their family, special friends, or even famous people they deem worthy. While in my life there are many worthy people to whom I might dedicate this book, my heart longs to honour My Loving Heavenly Father. Therefore, this book is dedicated to YeHoVaH, and to the furtherance of His great name throughout the world.
"May His name be sanctified[3]."
Matthew 6:9

---

[3] Translation of Matthew 6:9 by Nehemia Gordon & Keith Johnson from their book entitled, "A Prayer to Our Father"

TABLE OF CONTENTS

	Introduction	9
1	Heaven's Prophetic Picture	15

SECTION I:
OUTSIDE THE GATE

2	Heaven's Narrow Way	29
3	Heaven's True Perspectives	45
4	Heaven's Hidden Treasure	57
5	Heaven's Welcoming Promise	69

SECTION 2:
INSIDE THE GATE

6	Heaven's Challenge Embraced	83
7	Heaven's Message Expressed	95
8	Heaven's Majestic Reflection	109

SECTION 3:
INSIDE THE HOLY PLACE

9	Heaven's Peculiar Treasure	125
10	Heaven's Unshakeable Government	139
11	Heaven's Perfect Provider	149
12	Heaven's Watchful Eye	165

SECTION 4:
INSIDE THE THRONE ROOM

13	Heaven's Powerful Incense	179
14	Heaven's Interceding King	193
15	Heaven's Throne Room	205
16	Heaven's Prevailing Presence	221
	Conclusion	233

APPENDIX

About KJV	275
About the Author	281
A Name to Honour	256
Contact Information	283
Other Books by this Author	273
Salvation Message	267
Sinner's Prayer & Commitment	271
Scripture Index	276
Tabernacle Chapter Recap	264

INTRODUCTION

"Precious in the sight of the LORD is the death of his saints."

Psalm 116:15

In the normal process of life, people die, leaving behind this life, family and friends. Their survivors, especially those of a religious mindset, often wonder about the eternal destiny of the departed loved one. Did they make it to heaven? If so, what's it like there? What will they do there? Many questions flood their mind and unfortunately, may well go unanswered because Heaven, to most people, is a mystery. What little information people possess about heaven is usually limited to stories they heard from varied religious sources, or from those who claim to have experienced Heaven, perhaps from a momentary death, or an out-of-the-body experience and have come back to tell us about it.

Momentarily, try to collect some of your thoughts about heaven. How much information do you have? Can you assess the source of that information? Do you hold a mix of some non-biblical and biblical sources? If so, are you comfortable trusting in such? Or, perhaps, you're like me and you'd hesitate to accept what is not biblically verified. If so, you are sure to agree that when it comes to all spiritual matters, especially about our view of the afterlife, it is best if we have our information solidly based on truth. Such an important subject as our eternal destiny must rest on an unmovable foundation. When searching the unknown, its best to firmly fix our views on the One who never shifts or changes!

James 1:17
> 17 Every good gift and every perfect gift is from above, and cometh down from the Father of lights, with whom is no variableness, neither shadow of turning.

In considering the believer's handbook, the Bible, what facts are we told about heaven?

Does it tell us what to expect once we get there? Afterall, some people think they will sit on clouds, strum harps and rest quietly, in peaceful surroundings for all eternity. Is this biblical, or simply someone's imagination, or Hollywood's portrayal, at best? Will we relax and totally rest in eternity, or will we fulfil some assignment or service to God? What does the bible say, about our future life for all eternity?

Certainly, there are interesting passages giving us small glimpses into heaven's atmosphere. Isaiah, the prophet, for example, overwhelmed by a vision of the majesty of the Throne Room of heaven, humbly bowed before the Almighty, penitent, and ready to receive orders to go and preach God's Word.

In later books of scripture, we see more of the Throne Room, when, in the book of Revelation, the Apostle John is caught up into heaven. His record expands on the Throne Room scene. We're given glimpses of the Risen Saviour's glory, as well as aspects of worship activities in heaven, not to mention, future events to take place upon the earth. Yet, these amazing, inviting, and intriguing passages do not convey the totality of heaven. They merely crack the surface of the mystery and intrigue us even more! Surely, God wants us to know some answers. There must be passages answering questions of what "we" do, after we pass from this earth, *but* where are these passages?

"It's All About Heaven" stands ready to open the scriptures and show the reader God's powerful prophetic picture about heaven. This prophetic picture given by God, Himself, not only answers questions, but gives an idea of what to expect. However, this subject won't fit into the format of a quick read! Therefore, there's a workbook[4] with a mandate to that of an educator. It facilitates exploration of Bible passages about heaven to give a personal time between you, the reader, and the God you love.

Next, the textbook stands nearby as your companion on your personal journey to further unveil the prophetic picture as you discover much about heaven. With workbook and textbook in hand, through this inductive study method, your time with God aligns you to receive a trusted, biblical, knowledge of heaven.

---

[4] While a workbook is not mandatory, in our opinion, it facilitates greater learning, and gives opportunity for a much deeper experience with God.

Add that to the illuminating and penetrating power of the Holy Spirit, Who affirms the written Word and you'll see truth embedded into your life as an unshakable foundation upon which to stand.

Therefore, your approach, dear reader, is everything! If your mindset is to study this topic of heaven, *using this book as an instruction book to lead you to the scriptures*, that is a good beginning. Then as you put your heart and soul into this study, delving into the scriptures with worthy intensity, and you call upon the Holy Spirit to be your primary teacher and best friend *(which He desires to be)*, you should come away with a lot more than a working knowledge of heaven.

Your spiritual foundation, the one upon which you stand, if built and glued together with scripture and the Holy Spirit's staying power, will hold through the calm and through the storms. It will grow, and grow strong, even as you study and embrace the subject of heaven. Then, through all circumstances in life and when your life touches death, either your own or others, you should not waiver like blowing grass in the field. You should stand like a solid pillar for God wants you to be such in times of trouble, ready, willing, and able to share the truth of the scriptures to all in need.

Afterall, God wants you to know about eternity, for indeed, that is your destination. So, dear reader, in summary, "It's All About Heaven" is your open invitation to embark upon a spiritual journey, intended to explore the mystery of heaven. As you move towards that destination, you'll discover this study which incorporated your valuable time, produced numerous insightful and personal rewards. Your biblical peer into eternity will reveal, exactly, what the scriptures teach. Your faith and relationship with God must grow, too, as you discover that, today and onward to eternity, it's all about heaven!

HEAVEN'S PROPHETIC PICTURE

"See, saith he, that thou make all things according to the pattern shewed to thee in the mount."
Hebrews 8:5b

Heaven, with its unseen realm seems mysterious. Mysterious things are often hijacked by the imagination, escalating thoughts to realms unknown. While such a journey may prove exciting, when it comes to heaven, such ideas are only fodder for thought. These often produce uncertainty, fear, or doubt. These are no anchor for hard times such as when one faces eternity. On the contrary, believers need a firm foundation, upon which to stand. They need strong pillars to steady them as they walk through the deeper waters of life. So, let's ask ourselves a question, does our Christian manual, the Bible, take the mystery out of heaven?

Chapter 1 — Heaven's Prophetic Picture

Does the Bible talk about heaven?

While we won't find heaven's description in one specific passage, or even in a series of verses fixed in one place in the Bible, there is a revelation about heaven written in the Bible. Our Heavenly Father, YeHoVaH, the creator of all things, revealed heaven in a powerful prophetic picture, depicted a worship system, the layout of which replicates heaven. He gave this to Moses, an obedient prophet of YeHoVaH, who received and meticulously recorded that given revelation of heaven, and with great care oversaw the construction of its replica. We call that replica the Tabernacle of Moses. Have you heard of that Tabernacle? If so, did you know it shows a powerful picture of heaven?

Through this Bible Study, as we move towards our understanding of heaven, we'll unwrap the powerful, prophetic picture of heaven found in the Tabernacle of Moses. In doing so, we glean an understanding of heaven, and at the same time, enjoy the opportunity to explore the dynamics of heaven. When finished our study, we'll come away with a greater knowledge of our Heavenly Father, how to confidently approach Him, what He requires of us to enter eternity, and much more. We'll see His provision for us, now, as well as rewards and treasures for later. Together, as we study, we'll scripturally peer into the beauty of the sanctuary of Moses, which so exquisitely presents heaven in detail.

Now, to begin! Let's listen to YeHoVaH's instructions to Moses.

> Exodus 25:8-9
> 8 And let them make me a sanctuary; that I may dwell among them. 9 According to all that I shew thee, [after] the pattern of the tabernacle, and the pattern of all the instruments thereof, even so shall ye make [it]."

Using the word "pattern", in Exodus 25:8-9, we see that Moses must reproduce an exact model of the pattern that YeHoVaH showed Moses on the mount. Moses was not to get creative, nor make a partial copy of what he saw! YeHoVaH commanded Moses to make it exactly as he saw it, without any variation for that would mar the replica and shade the revelation that God intended. Its construction must, therefore, exclude human interpretation. The many specific aspects of heaven, namely, the understanding on how to reach, serve and walk with YeHoVaH, must have clarity, as well as the God-given way to access heaven. All these things dynamically unfold as our study progresses and we unwrap the biblical picture of heaven, as found in the Tabernacle of Moses.

In the past, Bible Studies on the Tabernacle of Moses showed a revelation of Yeshua, in every aspect including God's provided plan for mankind to enter heaven. Without a doubt, the Tabernacle of Moses clearly shows Yeshua in amazing ways, especially in defining salvation. Without salvation embracing God's way, no one comes before a holy God and spends an eternity with Him.

This pattern, from which Moses modelled the earthly tabernacle, carefully showed specific details, and the accompanying instructions of Moses, which is called the Torah[5], explained man's acceptable behaviour, as well as a plan for failed behaviour. Mankind needs these specifics, to understand how to reach, serve and walk with the God, who loved us so much that

---

[5] Torah means instruction.

He sent His only begotten Son, that whosoever believes in Him shall not perish[6].

Not only is defining sin, its consequences and God's provision for us, clearly seen in the Tabernacle, thus giving clarity to an otherwise obscure subject, but it goes one step further in that it defines heaven. This we will see, in stages as we study the biblical picture of heaven, as seen in the tabernacle and scriptures as Yeshua spoke about heaven.

YeHoVaH, in concern for us, showed us heaven, through this tabernacle because heaven has its mysteries, just like the ways that please God seemed mysterious to man. However, YeHoVaH, in mercy and love, revealed these mysteries to us through the prophets, in particularly, through Moses. Heaven, with its unseen realm likewise might be perceived as mysterious. Mysterious things can be hijacked by the imagination.

---

[6] "For God so loved the world, that he gave his only begotten Son, that whosoever believeth in him should not perish, but have everlasting life." John 3:16

When that happens, so many things are applied to the mind that are unrealistic. Fear, lies, deceptions and doubts come into play under these circumstances. Therefore, it makes perfect sense, that our loving heavenly Father, desired to give us a picture of heaven, upon which we can depend. He desired to remove the mystery out of heaven, in the same manner He removed the mystery out of knowing Him.

THE TABERNACLE LAYOUT
As we look at the tabernacle from a distance, we see it is surrounded by a fence. This fence is not incredibly tall, and certainly not indestructible, as it was made of linen. To enter beyond the walls into the complex, one must pass through a gate. Once through that one and only gate, one comes directly before a large, bronze Altar. Continuing forward moving toward the main building, one comes to a large, bronze basin, called a Laver.

After that comes the entrance to the actual Tabernacle, itself. Once inside the Tabernacle there were two Chambers, the first chamber was called, "The Holy Place". while the second was called "The Holy of Holies".

The entire Tabernacle of Moses, therefore, held three major sections:
- The section outside the fence, which totally separated or marked out of bounds, the entire area of the tabernacle from the world. Access by one gate only.
- The section immediately inside the fence, which stretches up from the inside of the fence and gate to the tabernacle (tent) itself,
- The section which includes the tabernacle (tent) with its two divisions, one named the Holy Place and the other, the Holy of Holies.

In summary, then, there are three major parts to the Tabernacle of Moses: Outside the Fence; Inside the Fence; and Inside the Tabernacle itself. Over the years, as people have studied this Tabernacle with its three major sections, they have given various interpretations to each section of the Tabernacle, including a picture it shows regarding the entrance.

Clearly, many teachings show this truth: as there is but one entrance into the Tabernacle area, *(through its one and only gate)*, there is but one entrance to heaven.

As people interpret the meaning of this prophetic picture of heaven, they remind believers that the gate, the one so colourfully and beautifully woven, represents Yeshua, who clearly stated, "I am the way the truth and the life",[7] and also said, "I am the door[8]". It is through Yeshua, and His teachings that we access the Father.

Regarding the Tabernacle then, its sole entrance way prophetically shows God's plan for mankind to enter heaven. YeHoVaH provided a way! Thus said, there is only *one way, and that is YeHoVaH's way*. Truly, that is an excellent and perfect interpretation of the gate!

In this study, we'll look at the main aspects of the Tabernacle of Moses, noting their application to the topic at hand, namely, Heaven. We will begin by examining the way God provided for entrance to the tabernacle, explaining, also, what is outside as well as inside the gate. Thus, we will divide this study into four (4) major sections:

---

[7] John 14:6 "Jesus saith unto him, I am the way, the truth, and the life: no man cometh unto the Father, but by me."
[8] John 10:7 "Then said Jesus unto them again, Verily, verily, I say unto you, I am the door of the sheep."

SECTION 1: OUTSIDE THE GATE
Here we'll look at the outer fence area and the gate. We'll call this area, **THE WORLD**.

In this section's 4 chapters, we'll look at discovering, assessing, valuing and finally, entering the gate.

Moving past this area, through the gate, which is none other than a clear picture of Yeshua, we'll enter the next area:

SECTION 2: INSIDE THE GATE:[9]
We'll call this area, **LIFE IN THE SPIRIT**
We'll explain this later, but for now, it is enough to know that the kingdom of God has a powerful influence upon this earth, and all true believers are part of that kingdom of God, here on earth. Also, we must remember the believer's position in Messiah, seated in heavenly places, and with an unrestrained ability to come before the throne of YeHoVaH.

---

[9] Shaded section in the diagram on the last page in this chapter.

Within this section, the three (3) chapters discuss THE BRAZEN ALTAR, with its challenges and message. Then, we'll look at THE LAVER.

Moving forward towards the tabernacle, we enter and see 2 chambers, the latter containing the ark.

SECTION 3: INSIDE THE HOLY PLACE
As we approach the Holy Place, we first must walk past 5 tall pillars, which hold a large veil in place. Only specially dedicated priests can move past that veil. As they move forward, they push aside the veil and walk into the first room of the tabernacle, itself. Within this place there are 3 specific items, namely the Menorah, the Table of Shewbread, and the Altar of Incense.

In this section, the first of five chapters highlights the believer's priesthood. The second chapter speaks about the 5 pillars and the veil; the third, fourth and fifth chapters depict the Table of Shewbread, the Menorah, and the Altar of Incense. Here, we'll learn to recognize the dealings of the government of the kingdom of YeHoVaH in operation, as well as heaven's view on the prayers of the saints, and YeHoVaH's provisional responses. Before moving into the second room of the Tabernacle, we encounter 4 tall pillars and another large veil, once again acting like a door. Into this special place only the High Priest could enter and at that, only once a year with a blood atonement for sins.

SECTION 4: INSIDE THE THRONE ROOM
This is the atmosphere of what many call, the 3rd heaven. Here is the representation of the very Throne Room of the Almighty. In this last section, we'll look at the Great High Priest, the 4 pillars & veil & the Ark of the Covenant. It is in this section that we'll look at heaven from the viewpoint of Worship around the throne.

PERSONAL REFLECTION:
Take some time and study the outline on the next page. Affix the layout in your mind as this is where we are going to head, throughout the chapters of this book. It is within this outline of the Tabernacle of Moses, where we'll embrace an understanding of God's prophetic picture of heaven in the scriptures, and what He desires us to know about Heaven[10].

---

[10] YeHoVaH's has reasons for what He does and *doesn't* tell us! Let's keep that in mind as we study!

OUTSIDE THE FENCE (The World)

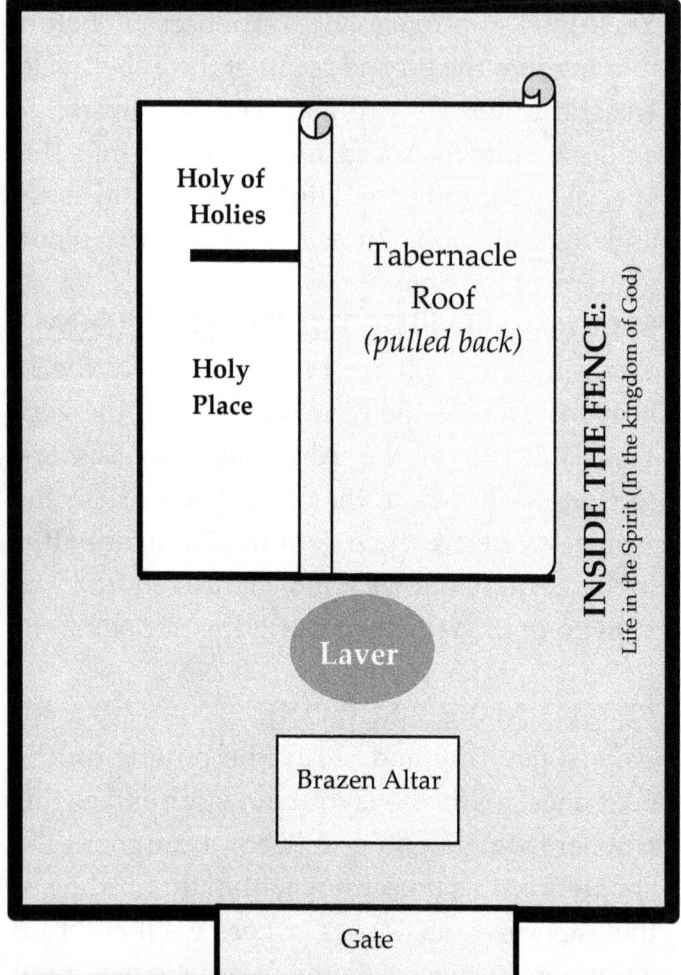

Later, as we study various scripture passages, you will see that Inside the Gate prophetically speaks of "life in the Spirit", while the Holy Place and the Holy of Holies, prophetically speaks of the THRONE ROOM.

SECTION 1: OUTSIDE THE GATE

THE GATE:
Discover it
Assess it
Value it
Enter it

HEAVEN'S NARROW WAY

"Then said the king to the servants, Bind him hand and foot, and take him away, and cast him into outer darkness; there shall be weeping and gnashing of teeth."

Matthew 22:13

As God depicted heaven to us, why did He include the world? Primarily, while we don't like to speak of it, nevertheless, it is true that not everyone who lives upon this earth, *and might even claim to know God,* really does know Him. Only those who truly are born of His Spirit accesses heaven for eternity. That fact is clearly mentioned in scripture, including within the teaching and parables of Yeshua.

God, therefore, in His picture of heaven, shows that there are those who live outside of the kingdom. This shows us, pictorially, that it is not a given for any person who dies to *immediately enter a wonderful eternity with God*. Rather, it clearly shows that once one passes away from this world to eternity, there is *no* **automatic entrance** *to an eternity with the Creator of all things.* Even though mankind is an offspring of Adam, one does not just naturally inherit heaven!

Our Bible is very clear that, for members of this human race to enter heaven's gate and thereafter spend an eternity with God, there are certain specifics, which must be met, amongst them, man must align with God's plans for their eternal existence to be with Him. Man does not call the shots in this regard! It is YeHoVaH's heaven, YeHoVaH's kingdom, YeHoVaH's home, and man must follow YeHoVaH's rules.

Still, in YeHoVaH's earnest desire to share heaven with us, He has given mankind choices. While upon this earth, we get to experiment with choices, hopefully concluding that it is better to do things YeHoVaH's way than our own! As we learn about YeHoVaH's ways, we learn that we can either gain heaven or be refused its eternal benefit. If we choose to make heaven's access a goal of this earth, and we decide to align our life to attain that goal, we open ourselves up to God's reality, or what is known as God's truth. However, we must come to that truth, on the terms of YeHoVaH.

On this exact thing, Yeshua commented:

John 14:6
> Jesus saith unto him, I am the way, the truth, and the life: no man cometh unto the Father, but by me.

Yeshua made it very clear, no one comes to the Father, except through Him. He is the way to the Father. He is the absolute truth, by which a person can access a good relationship here on earth with the Father[11], and eventually, enter YeHoVaH's eternity.

What is the sum of that truth? It is simply that man was created by God and put upon this earth to fulfil a purpose, part of which is to recognize an invitation to enjoy a two-sided relationship with the Creator and align ourselves accordingly. Should we accept God's invitation, from that time onward, we are to live

---
[11] YeHoVaH

our life embracing YeHoVaH, and adopt His ways.

Living life in this fashion makes heaven's goal more realistic; however, the truth is, that while it makes for a more fruitful experience upon this earth, it's not an easy life walking with God, by any means. Rather, it's a life that moves in tune with the Spirit of God, and thus, is lived out moment by moment with God at our side.

Living in this manner, we make ourselves more readily available for God's blessings as He defines them both here and in eternity. Things can be very predictable as we live out that life, here, but also, we must remember, such a life *goes against the main flow of the world*, and hence it has its turbulence to endure. Some of that turbulence, we'll speak of later.

If, while we're on earth, we make it a point to learn to develop an ear to hear what the Spirit of God speaks, we position ourselves to learn and receive from YeHoVaH's teachings. Clearly, the Spirit would have us embrace Yeshua's values on natural and spiritual things for these inherently contain vital information on how to attain our eternal destiny. As we receive what YeHoVaH's Spirit speaks, we discover that the greatest value upon this earth attained for eternity is YeHoVaH, Himself, and following that, the promised eternal life with Him.

Yet, there is another benefit, and it is for the here and now. We can access certain aspects of heaven's existence, from which we can function and operate, as we live out our life upon the earth. For those who truly believe, the existence and access to that existence is seen as an *invisible force*, (an invisible kingdom), with certain solid and effective principles affecting the earth. Yeshua called this invisible force "the kingdom of heaven" in some places, and "the kingdom of God" in others.

After our initial encounter with YeHoVaH, which should result in a true conversion experience, it is possible for us to understand, and fully embrace the many principles of God's kingdom, designed for the here and now. We learn how the kingdom of heaven affects us and others[12]. All principles operative in the

---

[12] This book addresses some of these things, especially in the second section of this book, entitled, "Inside the

kingdom of heaven begin at, and point to, its one and only access point: the gate, which is Yeshua. From that point onward, additional learning, like the entrance way, comes by choice, accessing by faith, what's available.

Information about functioning and operating within the kingdom of Heaven is expansion, and thus, too much for this opening section. Thus, this chapter speaks of the one- and only- way in, through the narrow gate. Indeed, it is as Yeshua said:

> Matthew 7:14
> 14 Because strait is the gate, and narrow is the way, which leadeth unto life, and few there be that find it.

In recording Yeshua's words from Matthew[13], in the Greek language, the word "narrow" implied more than just restricted. That same word, elsewhere, translators interpreted as afflict, or suffer tribulation:

Gate". In that section, we'll look at living life in the power of the Holy Spirit.

[13] There is ample evidence today that the gospel of Matthew was first written in Hebrew. For more information on that subject, research the internet, including such sites as sponsored by Michael Rood, or Nehemiah Gordon.

Narrow	2346	θλίβω thlibo thlee'-bo
		The word has an application to press hard upon, as one does with grapes to make wine. It can mean very narrow and contracted, or afflicted, troubled or distressed.
		Interpreted as trouble 4 x's, afflict 3 x's, narrow 1 x, throng 1 x, suffer tribulation 1 x.

One might ask what Yeshua really meant when He said the way was narrow, and furthermore, why the translators into Greek used the word they did? Is the narrow way capable of restricting one's movements? Is the way narrow, in the sense of pressured or squeezed, like a grape pressed for its juices? Was Yeshua telling us that the way to eternal life is filled with trials and tribulations?

One only needs to consider His Words elsewhere to know the answers to the above questions and to know exactly what He meant:

Matthew 16:24-25
24 Then said Jesus unto his disciples, If any man will come after me, let him deny himself, and take up his cross, and follow me. For whosoever will save his life shall lose it: and whosoever will lose his life for my sake shall find it.

Take up your cross to follow Yeshua sounds like trials and tribulations! Whosoever shall lose his life for Yeshua's sake shall find it, again, sounds like a very unpleasant experience, to say the least. Indeed, losing your life to gain the kingdom sounds like a narrow road!

Considering the narrow way described above, Yeshua's message to enter the kingdom is not an easy, painless, one step prayer and no more! His message highlights a strong-minded and resolute commitment to lay down our life and do so continually, moment by moment, for the remainder of our life here upon the earth. Thus, by losing our life for the cause of the kingdom, when this life is over, we'll then find eternal life. Such a life's description fits nicely in another parable of Yeshua's:

> John 12:24
> 24 Verily, verily, I say unto you, Except a corn of wheat fall into the ground and die, it abideth alone: but if it die, it bringeth forth much fruit.

A personal life, given to us to live out our own way, dies. That is the corn of wheat that falls into the ground and then dies, as we live the crucified life. If there is no death to self, there is no new life, for the corn of wheat needs to germinate, and in God's kingdom that germination process culminates in death to self. This is the life that produces much fruit!

While many today preach easy believism, those who truly understand the Words of Yeshua preach the reality of the narrow way into the kingdom for it requires a person's total, unwavering, follow-through to the end commitment. Listeners to preachers of truth are warned that it is a 100 per cent voluntary release of all personal rights to rule their own life. It is an intended bowing of the knee which willingly accepts the rulership of the Creator of the Universe.

Preachers, truly rooted in the depths of scriptural truth, convey to their listeners, that once in through the narrow way, life within continues through the choice of crucifixion of one's own wants and desires, to live out the will of YeHoVaH.

In YeHoVaH's scriptural truth, to choose to enter at the narrow gate, one chooses death to self. To stand and look at the narrow gate, to weigh out the cost to go through it and remain within it, is to truly perceive the pathway the scriptures describe:

Proverbs 4:20-27

"20 My son, attend to my words; incline thine ear unto my sayings. 21 Let them not depart from thine eyes; keep them in the midst of thine heart. 22 For they [are] life unto those that find them, and health to all their flesh. 23 Keep thy heart with all diligence; for out of it [are] the issues of life. 24 Put away from thee a froward mouth, and perverse lips put far from thee. 25 Let thine eyes look right on, and let thine eyelids look straight before thee. 26 Ponder the path of thy feet, and let all thy ways be established. 27 Turn not to the right hand nor to the left: remove thy foot from evil."

These scripture verses describe a very narrow way of life, as one keeps the Words of YeHoVaH ever before them, in the midst of their heart. According to the Proverbs 4 scripture recorded above, a forward mouth that speaks wickedness, gets its spring of water from the heart. Perverse lips that utter lies and deceptions finds its source within the heart. In accordance with scripture, then, we see that the choices of life originate in the heart[14].

---

[14] Matthew 15:19 Mark 17:21

It is within the depths of the heart, that we store energy for our words and actions. Therefore, scripture advises us to diligently keep the heart. We are commanded to watch over it, carefully, knowing what goes into our heart, meaning that upon which we meditate and hold dear, is that which directs the remainder of the body. The heart's domain is the body's source for thoughts, words, and actions.

A wise person keeps their eyes properly focused and centred along the paths laid out by YeHoVaH in the Word, not veering away, going neither to the right nor left. Hence, the pathway the foot treads upon receives its very direction which stems from the heart, thus establishing one's way to either keep or stray from the straight and narrow path. It is the heart and its stored wealth of treasures that directs the foot to walk towards doing good or evil. [15]

Summarizing these truths, then, in reference to the narrow way, if the person moves towards the narrow way and walks through it, their heart directed them to it. No credit is given to the heart here, but rather to the scriptures and to the Holy Spirit, Who presented, convicted

---

[15] Mark 7:20-23

and released the necessary power to walk in such a manner

Isaiah, the prophet said:

Isaiah 30:21
21 And thine ears shall hear a word behind thee, saying, This is the way, walk ye in it, when ye turn to the right hand, and when ye turn to the left.

Here, the lesson is to know and grasp that what the heart truly desires, is shown in the direction of life's pathway lived out. Certainly, YeHoVaH, leads and guides us by His Spirit to walk along the proper pathway. As a person searches for the proper pathway, scripture and its principles of life give voice to the matter of direction. On such a topic, Jeremiah said:

Jeremiah 6:16
16 Thus saith YeHoVaH, Stand ye in the ways, and see, and ask for the old paths, where is the good way, and walk therein, and ye shall find rest for your souls. But they said, We will not walk therein.

Again, this sounds a lot like what Yeshua said:

Matthew 11:28-30
    28 Come unto me, all ye that labour and are heavy laden, and I will give you rest. 29 Take my yoke upon you, and learn of me; for I am meek and lowly in heart: and ye shall find rest unto your souls. 30 For my yoke is easy, and my burden is light.

If mankind truly wants rest, if there is a passion for a rest, which only YeHoVaH gives, then it is found in the invitation of Yeshua. He'll set everyone free from the burden of doing things their own way, which normally amounts to heavy burdens, especially if the ideas of the way to heaven are impeded by so many "do's and don'ts of a religious system.

Yeshua's message is very simple, very basic, and very scriptural: "Enter in at the narrow gate". It may mean laying down those heavy burdens of life, things we impose upon ourselves. It may mean overcoming mindsets that have been set in place by religious training or philosophies. Surely, you've heard the teachings suggesting soon after we leave this world for the next, our good deeds are weighed against the bad. In this scenario, if good deeds comprise most of our life's actions, we receive admittance to spend eternity with YeHoVaH.

On the other hand, bad deeds exclude entrance. To receive Yeshua's teaching on heaven's entrance, some may find it necessary to abandon such theories!

In truth, any theories, no matter how popular or enthusiastically preached that do not properly align with scripture, must go! In their place, as we look at eternal life, wisdom embraces the words of Yeshua, for He clearly told us the Way. In fact, in accordance with His Words, (and the prophetic picture in the tabernacle of Moses), He is the Way as He said, and recorded for all time in John 14:6:

> 6 Jesus saith unto him, I am the way, the truth, and the life: no man cometh unto the Father, but by me.

This way into the kingdom could not be made clearer! It is coming to Yeshua, and as mentioned earlier, it is taking up our cross and following Him. To put that in real, down to earth, today's terms, it is this:
- Recognize that YeHoVaH & His ways are the right ways that lead to Eternal Life
- Desire to live for YeHoVaH, to have a relationship with Him and to please Him, making this your life's priority

- Lay down your entire life, giving it over to Him, to fulfil that purpose
- Receive Yeshua as Saviour and Lord[16]
- Live the crucified life from that point onward

Do this, and you've entered through the narrow way!

PERSONAL REFLECTION:
As you think about this chapter, give much thought to the concept of the Narrow Way. Perhaps, take pen and paper and outline in your own handwriting, what you perceive the narrow way requires from a person. What do you think someone must give up? How do you think a person needs to change their thinking? Do you think a person may need to change their own life's goals in order to fulfil their commitment to follow YeHoVaH? Then look and see if your conclusions fit with the words of Yeshua, including the latter part of the verse:

---

[16] If you don't know how to do this, read the message in the appendix on Salvation.

Matthew 7:14

> 14 Because strait is the gate, and narrow is the way, which leadeth unto life, and few there be that find it.

Dear Reader: We used this scripture earlier in this chapter, however, because of its importance we repeat it here. Contemplate taking time to look directly at your own life to see where you stand considering this scripture. Have you entered through the strait *(KJV for narrow)* gate? Do you walk the narrow way? Prayerfully, seek YeHoVaH to decide if you need to make any life's adjustments. Determine, with God's help, to do what is necessary!

HEAVEN'S TRUE PERSPECTIVE

"Again, the kingdom of heaven is like unto treasure hid in a field; the which when a man hath found, he hideth, and for joy thereof goeth and selleth all that he hath, and buyeth that field."
                                        Matthew 13:44

God's kingdom, both here and in eternity, is a priceless treasure. However, as we live upon this earth, first, we need to discover this fact, then embrace it, and thus, with God's enabling strength, be empowered to live within its principles. God's kingdom and its access to the believer is the greatest treasure given to mankind dwelling upon this earth!

Yeshua said, as seen in the opening scripture:

Matthew 13:44
> 44 Again, the kingdom of heaven is like unto treasure hid in a field; the which when a man hath found, he hideth, and for joy thereof goeth and selleth all that he hath, and buyeth that field.

In this parable, Yeshua relates His insights regarding the value of the kingdom of heaven, outlining how a person should perceive that kingdom. He relates this message by referring to a person's *material value* system. It seems apparent that most people wish to live well upon this earth. That focus often being the impetus and bottom line to many business deals Yeshua addresses the issue. He speaks of a certain man, who somehow discovered a field with a hidden treasure. That treasure, if owned by this man, promised him a better life.

In response to that possibility, the man went and sold everything in his possession, just to buy that field. His goal to have a better life, or to prosper in a great way, perceived that field with its hidden treasure, as greater worth than all he presently owned. In other words, his *future goal*, which focused on owning this field with its hidden treasure, was worth more in his eyes than all he presently owned. All his acquired wealth up to that point in time, seemed unimportant to him. Therefore, he sold all he had to buy this hidden treasure in a field.

In a very similar comparison Yeshua spoke this parable:

> Matthew 13:45 -46
> 45 Again, the kingdom of heaven is like unto a merchant man, seeking goodly pearls: 46 Who, when he had found one pearl of great price, went and sold all that he had, and bought it.

In this parable, we hear of a man, whose focus for income surrounded an art of buying goodly pearls. Goodly pearls are unmarred pearls, which are of great value, hold their value and eventually, even increase in value, too. Suddenly, the man discovers this special, and most likely, rare pearl. This pearl, he reasoned within himself, is worth everything and he absolutely must have it! Cost seemed unimportant!

Therefore, he liquidated his assets to buy this special pearl. Perhaps he sold his house and its contents, jewellery (including other pearls,) clothes, or shoes. Depending on the man's financial status at the time, his list of items he formerly treasured, might go on and on. Yet, as the man looked at the pearl, all he possessed, up to that point of time in his possession, seemed of lesser value than that which he absolutely must have! Thus, he takes everything tangible that he thus far gained in his life and sells it *just to buy* that *one treasure*!

In Yeshua's teachings of these two parables, we hear of one man who saw and then, valued *a hidden thing,* something not easily perceived, yet the man managed to know it was there. In the second parable, the man saw and valued something that his trained eye *saw*. In both parables, each man deemed the item of enough value to take and sell all they had, *meaning their total net worth*, in order to attain a new treasure. In the eyes of each purchaser, the item was a far better investment than *all they presently owned*. Their purchase was an investment, which in the long run, promised the greatest long-term remuneration.

In reflecting further on these two parables, the men, about which Yeshua spoke, were discerning businessmen. Note, the first parable speaks of a man who did not just hope there was a treasure within. He *knew* the treasure was in the field, even though *it was hidden*, and that's exactly why he bought it. In other words, this first parable speaks of a businessman who first perceived the hidden treasure and knowing it to have value, liquidated all his current assets to retain this one treasure as his own.

Yeshua, in presenting this man's behaviour to us, really presents him as one with foresight, or one possessing good business sense. This man was not like a man who bought a lottery ticket and hoped to win! No, this man planned to buy it. He had a strategy to follow and then followed through. That also shows a disciplined life as he dissolved his assets and acquired the new treasure. Summed up, this man weighed the cost. It cost him everything! He embraced the risks and the future benefits, and he acted in accordance with good business wisdom.

This same wisdom holds true of the man in the second parable, who bought a costly pearl. He, too, knew that value of the pearl, counted the cost of selling everything he owned to possess this one special pearl. Again, this purchase was not left to chance, it was not done with manipulation either. The man counted the cost, gladly paid it, and then attained the greater treasure, the most valued pearl.

These two parables, as well as their meaning, are summed up nicely in another important teaching of Yeshua:

> Matthew 6:21
> 21 For where your treasure is, there will your heart be also.

In applying principles from these two parables to our lives, we learn primarily that the greatest treasure upon this earth is recognizing the value of the kingdom of heaven and living in the light of it. Our focus on *that treasure* should rise above all things we may deem as other treasures. We should embrace the kingdom of heaven as the greatest value in our thoughts and actions. Thoughts of the kingdom, with its principles and requirements, should reign above all we strive to own and possess. In this light we thus perceive knowing YeHoVaH and consequently, walk through the strait gate and narrow gate (way) to eternal life[17]. To a true believer, this life and what it promises, must be worth everything!

If we embrace biblical perceptions of the principles of heaven and perceive heaven's goal as a priceless treasure, it is most likely that as we walk to attain it, we'll be extremely willing to pay the price, *which may cost us everything*! That sum of "everything" may include family, friends, jobs, reputation, freedom and ultimately, depending upon the circumstances in which we live, cost us all we hold dear, maybe even our very lives.

As Yeshua laid down His life for us, He made this statement on His way to the cross:

Luke 23:26-31
> 26 And as they led him away, they laid hold upon one Simon, a Cyrenian, coming out of the country, and on him they laid the cross, that he might bear it after Jesus.

---

[17] Matthew 7:14 Please note: It is two parts: the strait gate (your way in) and the narrow way (your walk inside the gate).

> 27 And there followed him a great company of people, and of women, which also bewailed and lamented him. 28 But Jesus turning unto them said, Daughters of Jerusalem, weep not for me, but weep for yourselves, and for your children. 29 For, behold, the days are coming, in the which they shall say, Blessed are the barren, and the wombs that never bare, and the paps which never gave suck. 30 Then shall they begin to say to the mountains, Fall on us; and to the hills, Cover us. 31 For if they do these things in a green tree, what shall be done in the dry?

Here, we see Yeshua paying the price for our Eternal Life. We see Him, even in great agony of body, speaking to the women so troubled by His ordeal. To them, He prophesies a time when a barren womb is a blessing, rather than a curse. He speaks of a distress so great, that people, if possible, would call for the mountains to fall on them, for the hills to cover them.

Even in His pain as He endured His horrific death circumstances, His compassion for others reached out. If they killed the Son of Man, in this green season, *the time of God's favour on His*

People, how horrible for the days coming when He is gone, and the dry season arrives! Yeshua's prophetic eyes see ahead to the day when Jerusalem was surrounded and besieged by her enemies. Then, the fruitful women would groan within themselves at what they and their children faced. Then, as distress arise to great heights, those alive wished they were dead.

Here, Israel's eyes, was a treasure they did not perceive: *Yeshua!* Here was a pearl of great price they did not recognize nor want to keep. Their rejection of the greatest treasure of the Almighty did result in a dry season, which brought forth great tribulation and much death. God's mercy, however, shortened those days, for the sake of the elect:

Matthew 24:19-22

> 19 And woe unto them that are with child, and to them that give suck in those days! 20 But pray ye that your flight be not in the winter, neither on the sabbath day: 21 For then shall be great tribulation, such as was not since the beginning of the world to this time, no, nor ever shall be. 22 And except those

days should be shortened, there should no flesh be saved: but for the elect's sake those days shall be shortened.

Looking at this instance, prophetically, (even past the second fulfilment of this prophecy) the green season *is our time* to receive from heaven. It *is our time*, here upon earth, when we can look at eternal life, as God presents it and then, make our choice.

If we don't perceive heaven's treasure and consequently, don't make the proper advancements to secure that treasure, we enter a spiritual dry season where eventual death awaits. Indeed, Yeshua groaned at such agony awaiting Israel, and certainly the Heavenly Father groans at those who toss out the most valuable treasure of the kingdom. It is far better to agree with God's Word, then, accept the treasure, here and now.

To put it figuratively, matching the parable, it is great wisdom to sell all one has in their possession, *(die to self)* to follow Yeshua and embrace the way He set in place for them, *(crucifixion)*, than to breeze through this life with an easy commitment to God, so easily abandoned or set aside for the moment, and in the end, come face to face with eternal death.

Regarding heaven and its true perspective, the Torah, the Prophets, and the Writings make it clear: *there is nothing in this world that one could earn, possess, invest in, or experience,* ***which is of greater value than the kingdom of heaven.*** Surely, when it is perceived as such, nothing dims in its light, not even under persecution for one's faith: *"Blessed are they which are persecuted for righteousness' sake: for theirs is the kingdom of heaven*[18]*."*

Matthew 5:10

PERSONAL REFLECTION:

As you finish up this chapter, please take some time and ask YeHoVaH to give you further insight as to your own *personal priorities* to see if they align with Heaven's. Perhaps, as a suggestion, you might ask YeHoVaH questions like:
- Do spiritual matters take priority in my own life?

---

[18] Please note, "theirs is the kingdom of Heaven" because these people are already in the kingdom and following the righteous ways of YeHoVaH that they are persecuted. Remember, it is not that they receive the kingdom due to persecution for their righteousness.

- Do I care about the spiritual destiny of others?
- Do I keep silent, or do I speak to others about their eternal destiny, in and out of season[19]?
- Am I totally sold out to follow the one, who died in my place, obeying the scriptures?

Whatever questions come to mind as you seek YeHoVaH, take your time, and simply allow the Holy Spirit to help you in an assessment of where you are now and the direction in which you intend to go, in the future. Allow the Spirit to help you lay it all before Him, surrendering everything to His capable hands.

---

[19] Opportunities are not always convenient, but do you follow the prompting of the Holy Spirit and share as He leads?

HEAVEN'S HIDDEN TREASURE

YeHoVaH is exalted; for he dwelleth on high: he hath filled Zion with judgment and righteousness. And wisdom and knowledge shall be the stability of thy times, and strength of salvation: the fear of YeHoVaH is his treasure.

Isaiah 33:5-6

Upon this earth, as mankind lives and walks through it, each person has choices to make. Some of those choices include attitudes on possessing treasures while upon the earth. Many people, in their mind's eyes, perceive their time here as all important and give no place to thoughts of an afterlife.

There are those who live only for the collection of physical or earthly treasures, and likewise, some, those who we tag as atheistic, live for only the here and now, denying the existence of any God to Whom they are accountable. To these people, in the last moments of their life as eternity stares them in the face, the philosophies they embraced, as well as those things for which they spent a lifetime collecting, suddenly leave them comfortless, fleeing away, totally useless in eternity.

Keeping that in mind, there is a rather cute story[20] about a man who spent his entire life striving for earthly gold. In the story, he dies, and as he passes from this world to the next, he was granted a wish to take with him something that was extremely important to him. Thinking with his worldly mind, he stuffs some pure gold coins into his pocket. This gold is worth a great deal of money, and in the man's mind, represents something he didn't want to leave behind.

Arriving at heaven's gate, the man is met by an angelic being. "Sir", says the angel, "before you enter heaven, can you tell me your life's greatest treasure." Smiling, the man puts his hand into his pocket and pulls out an abundance of gold

---

[20] Source of the story not known.

coins. Then, with a broad smile, proudly declares this as his greatest treasure.

Looking very puzzled, the angel takes his hand and pushes open a very large door. As the door opens wide, the man gets a glimpse of heaven, and that great city of gold. "What's that I see shining on the streets of that great city?" inquires the man. "Don't you know? "The angel replies, "it is pure gold, like you pulled out of your pocket. "So, tell me," says the angel, looking rather puzzled," "Why would anyone bring a piece of pavement *here?*"

Of course, this story is not biblical but rather told to provoke one's thinking regarding life's focus. The moral of the story looks past the reality of the gold pavement in heaven,[21] to focus on the vast difference between heaven's treasures and those of the earth.

Biblically speaking, any person who pursues *only life's worldly treasures,* has their life's value system totally out of focus.

---

[21] Revelation 21:21 And the twelve gates were twelve pearls; every several gate was of one pearl: and the street of the city was pure gold, as it were transparent glass.

However, the question does remain, are there treasures on earth that man can pursue that affect the afterlife? On this topic, Yeshua commented:

Matthew 6:19-21
> 19 Lay not up for yourselves treasures upon earth, where moth and rust doth corrupt, and where thieves break through and steal: 20 But lay up for yourselves treasures in heaven, where neither moth nor rust doth corrupt, and where thieves do not break through nor steal: 21 For where your treasure is, there will your heart be also.

It is obvious, by this scripture, there are treasures one can pursue upon this earth, which are not stored in treasure boxes here, but rather are stored in heaven. Pursuing after those treasures results in eternal value, since nothing gained for heaven will end up stolen, rusted or corrupted.

Those who genuinely have faith understand that the treasures about which Yeshua spoke are not those of gold and silver, nor of any form of temporal value. In other words, Yeshua's message clearly points out there is a higher focus than what's right in front of us. To obtain such a focus, we need to look at where our heart lies. For example, do we seek God's wisdom as we choose our values to pursue, values about which the scriptures speak? Such values might include a good name, wisdom, and fear of YeHoVaH, to name a few. These are treasures beyond earth's value!

A GOOD NAME:

Proverbs 22:1
1 A good name is rather to be chosen than great riches, and loving favour rather than silver and gold.

When one's choice is to have a good name, one looks past the moment and its pleasures, past the approval or disapproval of their immediate peers. In the above scripture, such a person, focuses on more than great riches, silver or gold which satisfy them, now. Perhaps, to the world and its values, a person may be scorned, ridiculed, or even hated, and their name held in distain, but the true weighing of the matter is this: *in God's eyes, how are they seen?*

As an example, let's look at Yeshua. As we read about His life in the scriptures, we see that He made a continual choice to do the right thing, even when others scorned Him and said all manner of evil against Him. Yet, Yeshua chose to follow the pathway of YeHoVaH. That pathway led to a cruel, shameful and excruciating death, alongside two criminals, who for their life's choices, were condemned to death. After Yeshua's humiliation, death, burial and resurrection, YeHoVaH gave Him a name above all names:

Philippians 2:5-9
5 Let this mind be in you, which was also in Christ Jesus: 6 Who, being in the form of God, thought it not robbery to be equal with God: 7 But made himself of no reputation, and took upon him the form of a servant, and was made in the likeness of men: 8 And being found in fashion as a man, he humbled himself, and became obedient unto death, even the death of the cross. 9 Wherefore God also hath highly exalted him, and given him a name which is above every name:

Truly Yeshua taught us a lesson, with His own death, that it is far better to follow the will of YeHoVaH, no matter the cost and to receive God's approval, then to opt out for man's approval, which is at best, a temporary reward. Yeshua clearly showed that His treasure was in heaven, wherein was His focus!

WISDOM

Proverbs 3:13-18
13 Happy is the man that findeth wisdom, and the man that getteth understanding. 14 For the merchandise of it is better than the merchandise of silver, and the gain thereof than fine gold. 15 She is more precious than rubies: and all the things thou canst desire are not to be compared unto her.16 Length of days is in her right hand; and in her left hand riches and honour.17 Her ways are ways of pleasantness, and all her paths are peace.18 She is a tree of life to them that lay hold upon her: and happy is every one that retaineth her.

Here wisdom is shown as a great prize, a treasure worth more than silver or fine gold. Wisdom is seen as more precious than a ruby, a very valuable gem of that day. Nothing is more precious, the author uttered under Divine inspiration, than wisdom for, in modern terms, it surpasses anything than one desires! A pursuit for wisdom satisfies, and results in a tree of life for those who grab hold. Happy is that person's lot if they keep wisdom!

FEAR OF YEHOVAH

> Proverbs 15:16
> 16 Better is little with the fear of YeHoVaH than great treasure and trouble therewith.

> Psalm 111:10
> "The fear of YeHoVaH [is] the beginning of wisdom: a good understanding have all they that do [his commandments]: his praise endureth for ever.")

These two Bible verses are simple in their message. In this life, it is better to keep the pursuit of worldly values as small, as an unimportant priority, than to do the reverse and overlook a higher focus: *the fear of YeHoVaH*.
This is a far better priority. That "fear of YeHoVaH" means no acquiring of goods or

creature comforts by means of fraud, damaging others, bypassing God's ordinances, statutes, and commandments. It means to do all things properly, decently and in God's order, rather than to evade these things in order to obtain great wealth.

This fear of YeHoVaH is a priceless treasure for which one should seek. Here, the bottom line, is to develop an awareness of one's accountability to YeHoVaH, and in doing so, embrace all His ways of righteousness. In the end, the wise person knows and understands that YeHoVaH, alone, weighs a person's deeds, as well as all intentions. If one considered the approval of YeHoVaH as a treasure, it indeed would be life's treasure hunt, producing value of immeasurable worth!

MORE TREASURES

Scripture gives us many more treasures, but these few sufficiently convey the message. Our value system, the one by which we live, determines our life's goals, how we obtain those goals, and eventually, the lasting and eternal honour which is afforded to us. When our focus is YeHoVaH and His approval, we set our life's goal to reflect our heart's desire: to please God rather than man.

Defining our life's goals, *(as noted earlier)* and outlining our value system all goes back to Yeshua's words,

> Matthew 6:21
> 21 For where your treasure is, there will your heart be also.

If we pursue the things of God upon this earth, we may or may not receive monetary and personal rewards, as the presence or absence of these do not determine God's pleasure in us. Rather, God's pleasure in us is determined by our obedience to His will, in all things. Our eyes, when heaven bound, must remain fixed on heaven's rewards, for that is where the greatest treasures lay, if indeed that is where we focus our heart! Of course, as said earlier, that does not mean we cannot enjoy earthly goods, but those earthly goods come as God blesses.

These treasures are not gained by manipulation or fancy words set out to manoeuvre valued goods out of the hands of others, so that we might prosper. They are merely early tokens of

God's rewards, in the here and now, that arrive in our life to help us obtain further goals of heaven. These visual treasures are not added to our life to build a larger pile of earthly treasures, [22] nor are they to become weights to tie us down. They are not to become decoys or idols to draw us away from heaven's hidden treasure and our truest treasure.

Todays' treasures are none of those things!

Rather, earthly treasures stand as ready assets to use for the furtherance of heaven's goals, assets to liquify if necessary, for the work of the kingdom of God! Life's goals are paramount, and as we know, dear reader, certain things are common to all mankind, and one of those things is death. According to scripture, following life's end, comes judgment:

Hebrews 9:27
27 And as it is appointed unto men once to die, but after this the judgment:

---

[22] Luke 12:20 But God said unto him, Thou fool, this night thy soul shall be required of thee: then whose shall those things be, which thou hast provided?

2 Corinthians 5:10
> 10 For we must all appear before the judgment seat of Christ; that everyone may receive the things done in his body, according to that he hath done, whether it be good or bad.

Whether one believes this or not, is not the point. Atheists, agnostics, as well as believers shall stand before the Judgment seat to give an account of what they've done in the flesh. Scripture clearly tells us,

Jeremiah 17:9-10
> 9 The heart is deceitful above all things, and desperately wicked: who can know it? 10 I, YeHoVaH, search the heart, I try the reins, even to give every man according to his ways, and according to the fruit of his doings.

Better to give this dilemma to YeHoVaH, today. Let's not allow a deceitful heart to guide us through life and into a dark, foreboding and unreceptive eternity.

PERSONAL REFLECTION
As this first chapter closes, dear reader, please reflect upon your *personal life's values*. How do

you perceive your time upon this earth? What are your life's goals? What are your life's greatest treasures? Are you ready to face eternity?

Chapter 4   Heaven's Hidden Treasure

HEAVEN'S WELCOMING PROMISE

"The highway of the upright is to depart from evil: he that keeps [23]the way of YeHoVaH preserves his soul."

Proverbs 16:17

Now that we understand from scripture, that the kingdom of heaven is the greatest treasure upon this earth for which man can pursue and obtain, [24] we're going to look at the entrance way in a little more detail than we did in the first chapter. We'll do this because it is very important to ensure that we understand, embrace and absolutely follow the basics. In

---

[23] KJV reads "his way", however, to make clear reference to the way the author intends, the words "the way of YeHoVaH's" replaced "his way"

[24] We studied this in an earlier chapter.

order to live a "life in the Spirit', we must ensure we are totally in the kingdom of YeHoVaH. We must be certain that we have YeHoVaH's Spirit living within, for there is no other way to walk in the Spirit!

Yeshua spoke much about the entrance into the kingdom of heaven. He taught that to enter the kingdom of heaven one's righteousness must exceed that of the religious leaders of His day, known as the scribes and Pharisees[25].

Furthermore, Yeshua taught that not every one that calls Him Lord will enter the kingdom of heaven. That welcoming entrance is limited to the ones that do the will of the Father which is in heaven[26]. While these two scriptures speak volumes, to which we will return to look at later, perhaps the most famous passage found in the Apostolic scriptures regarding heaven's entrance is found in John Chapter 3:

In the opening scene of John Chapter 3, a teacher named Nicodemus comes to Yeshua. He relates an astute observation to Yeshua:

---

[25] Matthew 5:20
[26] Matthew 7:21

John 3:2b
"We know that thou art a teacher come from God: for no man can do these miracles that thou doest, except God be with him."

In response to this comment, Yeshua makes a profound statement, which gives Nicodemus a lot to think about:

John 3:3-8
3 Jesus answered and said unto him, Verily, verily, I say unto thee, Except a man be born again, he cannot see the kingdom of God. 4 Nicodemus saith unto him, How can a man be born when he is old? can he enter the second time into his mother's womb, and be born? 5 Jesus answered, *Verily, verily, I say unto thee, Except a man be born of water and of the Spirit, he cannot enter into the kingdom of God*[27]. 6 That which is born of the flesh is flesh; and that which is born of the Spirit is spirit. 7 Marvel not that I said unto thee, Ye must be born again. 8 The wind bloweth where it listeth, and thou hearest the sound thereof, but canst not tell whence it cometh, and whither it

---

[27] Kingdom of Heaven (same thing).

goeth: so is every one that is born of the Spirit.

Since Nicodemus believed and just stated that Yeshua came from God[28], Yeshua went right to the task of addressing a key aspect of the kingdom of God, (Heaven). *"Except a man be born again, he cannot see[29] the kingdom of God".*

Taking Yeshua's comment literally, Nicodemus replied with two rhetorical questions: How can a man be born when he's old? Can he enter a second time into his mother's womb and be born?

Yeshua probably smiled at this comment, since the answer was an obvious no. Then, He made His message clearer, "except a man[30] (person) is born of water and of Spirit, he cannot enter into the kingdom of God". Yeshua, knowing that

---

[28] John 3:2b

[29] Scholars today debate the Greek word used here for "see", Strong's concordance 1492 οιδα oida oy'-da or ειδω eido i'-do. Word interpreted as-know, cannot tell, know how, see, behold, look, perceive, know

[30] The use of the term man here is a generic word used often to mean the whole of mankind, and likewise, the pronoun "he", which follows. These principles are not gender specific, but rather apply to all humankind!

mankind understands the spiritual world through a comparison to the physical, [31] helped Nicodemus to look for a deeper meaning in His earlier comments. Yeshua's next comment made a clear distinction between the natural things of this earth and the spiritual world around us:

"That which is born of the flesh is flesh; and that which is born of the Spirit is spirit."[32]

Yeshua then took Nicodemus one step further towards understanding of the kingdom of God: "Marvel not that I said unto you, you must be born again. The wind blows where it desires, and you hear the sound thereof, but cannot tell from where it came, or where it goes. So is everyone born of the Spirit." [33]

Nicodemus, as a teacher of Israel; was most likely exposed to, or perhaps even officiated in baptizing proselytes into the Jewish faith.

---

[31] "For the invisible things of him from the creation of the world are clearly seen, being understood by the things that are made, [even] his eternal power and Godhead; so that they are without excuse:" Romans 1:20.
[32] John 3:6
[33] John 3:7-8

According to some resources available today, when a proselyte was baptized, as they came out of the running water to the other side of the mikvah, the baptizing official cried out "born again". If Nicodemus knew this, it is apparent from his comments that he didn't get its full symbolism.

When one repents, leaves their sins behind, immersing themselves into the moving waters, they show the past washed or carried away by the running waters. This is the fulfilment of heaven's welcoming promise: *born again!* Emphasizing that point, as they arise out of the water, they prophetically declare their new life. Indeed, they are a new person! The old life lived *for self* has passed away. Now, they live their life *for God*. They live for righteousness and holiness. They live to please God, not man, and certainly not themselves![34]

Whether Nicodemus understood this before or after his conversation with Yeshua we do not know, but we can understand this as we have access to the Apostolic scriptures, which explain

---

[34] 2 Corinthians 5:17 Therefore if any man be in Christ, he is a new creature: old things are passed away; behold, all things are become new.

it. We know that baptism, which follows conversion, demonstrates repentance of sin, and an abandoning of one's old life to follow God, with all their heart, mind, soul, and strength.

One who enjoys a genuine conversion, is a new creation, entering a totally new life, serving God. They have died from their old life of serving themselves and now their focus is to live out their purpose in alignment with the will of God, and His kingdom. In other words, they have enjoyed a new birth, and now have a new life. They are now starting over, born again.

Over the years, especially in the light of the prosperity Gospel, this message of being born again has lost much of its original meaning, buried or even perhaps excluded, due to the use of modern ideas and philosophies. Easy believism has often taken the place of a call to embrace a life of complete abandonment to one's own life of living for self, in order to embrace the total will, plans and purposes of the One who redeemed them.

In other words, they have chosen a new life with its total abandonment to all they were in the past, and all their plans for their future, as they must now come to an end, for the purpose of their higher calling.

What they now are to consider and learn to live out are things designed by God, which further advance the kingdom of God; things which exalt and uplift the Creator; things which manifest by the power of God as these individuals now walk out their new life on a totally different foundation than before. This means, they abandon, without reservation, the laws, rules and regulations of their former life and all expressions of self that it entailed, and move forward to embrace the laws, rules and regulations of the kingdom of light, the kingdom of YeHoVaH.

This is the life Yeshua spoke about, as He talked with Nicodemus. This is the life Yeshua meant by the words,

John 3:5
> *Verily, verily, I say unto thee, Except a man be born of water and of the Spirit, he cannot enter into the kingdom of God*[35].

---

[35] Kingdom of Heaven (same thing)

Are you beginning to see that entrance into the kingdom of heaven is not about tomorrow? Do you see it's about today and choices made right now? It is from this earth we enter the kingdom of God, and thus align ourselves for heaven. This is Yeshua's point! His thoughts were on eternity. Changes made here are crucial, specially to the life God expects us to live today, for true life is not a life lived in the flesh, but only in the Spirit.

John 3:6
> 6 That which is born of the flesh is flesh; and that which is born of the Spirit is spirit.

Indeed, it can only be in the Spirit that one fully lives the life that God has called us to live in Messiah. Those that are born of the Spirit, and move with the Spirit, are just as Yeshua described:

John 3:7
> 7 Marvel not that I said unto thee, Ye must be born again. 8 The wind bloweth where it listeth, and thou hearest the sound thereof, but canst not tell whence it cometh,

and whither it goeth: so is every one that is born of the Spirit.

PERSONAL REFLECTION:
It is at this point, dear reader, we will end this chapter so you may take time to reflect upon your experience in Messiah. As you think about the definition of born again, as this chapter outlined it, see if you fit within that description. See if you remember a former life of repetitive sin that, *for you is past,* with the *primary focus of self and its wants and ambitions gone.* Do you know a new life that embraces the things of the kingdom of God, the kingdom of heaven?

If you wish to look further into this subject, spend some time with YeHoVaH and ask Him to help you mark where you stand with Him. It is imperative that you get this aspect of heaven's principles, ensuring it is a reality in your life. Then, you will know for sure you've entered heaven's Gates and are on the right road to living an eternity with YeHoVaH.

SECTION 2:
INSIDE THE GATE

THE BRAZEN ALTAR:
Embrace it
Communicate it
THE LAVER:
Utilize it

HEAVEN'S CHALLENGE EMBRACED

"I beseech you therefore, brethren, by the mercies of God, that ye present your bodies a living sacrifice, holy, acceptable unto God, which is your reasonable service."

Romans 12:1

As one enters inside the gate, the first thing seen is a large bronze Altar upon which priests offered sacrifices. Prophetically speaking, this Altar shows Calvary and Yeshua's life as He gave His all, willingly pouring out His life to redeem mankind. Of Yeshua's attitude we are told in Hebrews:

Hebrews 12:2
>   2 Looking unto Jesus the author and finisher of our faith; who for the joy that

was set before him endured the cross, despising the shame, and is set down at the right hand of the throne of God.

In this scripture, see Yeshua's kind of love, His faithfulness to His Father, and His total dependence upon His Father. This type of commitment, this absolute abandonment of one's will to follow the Father's will, can't be expressed by mere words. Somehow, the words awesome, inspiring or moving all fall incredibly short.

While Hebrews 12:2 gives us glimpses into Yeshua's abandonment to do YeHoVaH's will, there is a passage in the gospel of Luke which shares more intimate details of Yeshua's submission to the will of His Father:

> Luke 22:41-44
> 41 And he was withdrawn from them about a stone's cast, and kneeled down, and prayed, 42 Saying, Father, if thou be willing, remove this cup from me: nevertheless, not my will, but thine, be done. 43 And there appeared an angel unto him from heaven, strengthening him. 44 And being in an agony he prayed more

earnestly: and his sweat was as it were great drops of blood falling down to the ground.

In Hebrews 12:2, Yeshua's focus described as "the joy set before Him", portrays His gaze which looked past the shame, brutality and pain of the cross and looked forward to the joy of the eventual reunion or homecoming of Yeshua into His Father's forever presence. Luke 22:41-44 shows His fleshly desire to have the situation turn in another direction, *if possible*.

This inquiry of Yeshua's shows that His flesh preferred another plan, yet, even if that was not possible, Yeshua would do it the Father's way. Later, after the horrors of His death, burial and then the joy of His resurrection, Yeshua received His great reward. He is now sitting at the right hand of the throne of YeHoVaH, and there, according to Hebrews 7:25 He intercedes for us.

Hebrews 7:25
> 25 Wherefore he is able also to save them to the uttermost that come unto God by him, seeing he ever liveth to make intercession for them.

Surely, having conquered the conflict between flesh and Spirit, our Heavenly Intercessor is ready to help us, any way we need it. Yeshua's work on the cross, and the demands of His flesh to follow God's will was not generated by the flesh. Such *total abandonment* was only generated by the Holy Spirit, who helped Yeshua to complete His heavenly assignment. This the scriptures tell us:

Hebrews 9:14
> 14 How much more shall the blood of Christ, who through the eternal Spirit offered himself without spot to God, purge your conscience from dead works to serve the living God?

As through the Eternal Spirit Yeshua offered himself as that spotless Lamb, likewise, we must learn to lean upon the Spirit to help us live out our life, with the sole purpose of existing to complete the Father's will, in every situation. As we walk toward that direction of serving YeHoVaH as a living sacrifice, our flesh constantly must give way to the promptings of the Holy Spirit, as we hear His word and obey it. For those who truly believe, moving forward past the gate and staring right into the brazen

Altar, can only mean a life as outlined in Romans 12:1:

> 1 I beseech you therefore, brethren, by the mercies of God, that ye present your bodies a living sacrifice, holy, acceptable unto God, which is your reasonable service.

Here, in his letter to the saints at Rome, Paul makes it very clear that those in Messiah are "living sacrifices", just as Yeshua was a living sacrifice for us. This lifestyle, which includes a total abandonment to YeHoVaH, shows our oneness in Messiah and are sincere entrance into the kingdom of God. We walk forward with a focus on the "joy set before us", which means embracing YeHoVaH's total plans and purposes for our life, always yielded to His will, and in all things. In the words of the Apostle Paul, this is our reasonable service.

Yes, from our new birth experience, moving forward, into our new life in God, we truly live *only* by dying to our own will, forsaking all that we desire, in exchange for embracing the will of Yehovah and what He desires on our behalf. To the untrained ear, this might sound terrible! To the one taught *only* in the school of easy believism, it might seem appalling, cruel and untrue. However, we must embrace the life before us, *and the holy One to Whom we're enjoined,* by living *a life of abandonment to our own way of doing things.* God is not a cruel nor sadistic Master! What He asks of us is doable. It's not designed on a whim nor established to make us jump through hoops! Rather, YeHoVaH's desire for us to live yielded to His will is designed as a blessing producing great rewards, *even if it costs* the undoing of our flesh and its desires.

YeHoVaH is a loving, caring, Heavenly Father, and as such, His will for us is defined by that which is good for us. It may not seem so in the immediate moment, but in the eventual dispensation of God's time for our lives, it will produce good fruit and immeasurable rewards. Ours is to look past the moment! Ours is to rest in YeHoVaH and His pleasure in us as we do our best to live our lives before Him in the way that He chooses.

YeHoVaH's will, whether we know it immediately or sometime in the future, embraces only things designed to bring us into a greater fulfilment in life, here, as we fulfil our purpose, and will have a future reward as well. Regarding that purpose, we might immediately recognize it, or as seems more common, feel it is hidden from our understanding, with glimpses or hints of it, here and there. One might recognize a call, be drawn towards a certain aspect of life's fulfilment, yet not clearly understand the final goal. That being the case, it is still a very biblical way of going through life.

Young Joseph, on his way to Egypt, sold as a slave by his unloving and shrewd brothers, entered an irreversible pathway to his destiny, *to his life's purpose*. That destiny or purpose lay hidden, even though earlier prophesied in dreams.[36] Joseph's destiny, fulfilled, saved every person in his father's household. Whether Joseph knew it, or if it was totally concealed from his eyes, God's watchful eye kept him, and YeHoVaH never left his side!

Genesis 50:20
20 But as for you, ye thought evil against me; but God meant it unto good, to bring

---

[36] Genesis 37:7 and surrounding verses shows one such prophetic dream.

to pass, as it is this day, to save much people alive.

So, like Joseph, we face our destiny, hidden or exposed. As we do, we live every moment to please YeHoVaH, looking forward to the pleasure of pleasing Him. As we do that, we fulfil our reasonable service, as well as fulfil whatever is necessary in God's plan for our eternal life.

Afterall, YeHoVaH is an eternal being and His amazing strategies and awesome purposes encompass eternal value! God's plans and purposes are never just for the moment! If we are sold out to the things of the kingdom of God, we are, indeed, His faithful servants. Therefore, individually, on that appointed day, we'll hear those powerful and longed-for words: *"well done thou good and faithful servant."*

We see this truth echoed in the parables that Yeshua taught, such as the parable found in Matthew 25, and a very similar parable found in Luke 19[37].

---

[37] For the purpose of this part of the textbook, we will refer to the story in Matthew 25.

As we explore certain verses in Matthew Chapter 25[38], we see the activities of a certain man who went into a far country. Prior to his journey, he called his servants, and he divided his goods amongst them, entrusting it to each servant, as he believed each one could handle. Then, he went away on his journey.

As time went by, the master returned home. In his first task, he set out to assess what was done with his goods in his absence. He called his servants before him. As he did, it was discovered that the one who received five talents managed to add another five talents. He doubled the master's property! Very pleased, the master rewarded this servant with words of praise and a position of power. The next servant was also found to have doubled the master's goods. He, also, was praised, and given a position of power.

Soon, we hear of the one who received the least of the master's property. He dug a hole in the earth and hid what the master entrusted to him. He presented the master his own goods with an elaborate explanation of the character of the master. The master was very angry with that

---

[38] Matthew 25:14-30

servant, for that servant did not see the value of what the master entrusted to him. Instead, he made a judgment of the master's character. In addition, since he did not want to add to his master's treasures, he simply did what he thought was best. In other words, he did his own thing! Obviously, the master knew this servant was capable of doubling what was given to him, yet he chose to do nothing with it. In the end, the servant was called wicked and thrown outside the kingdom. [39]

In looking at this story, it is easy to recognize that we are servants of the Most High God. We've been entrusted with many things, including the powerful Holy Spirit that lives within. Will we yield to the Spirit? Will we bring forth fruit unto the kingdom of God or will we do what the wicked servant did and bury the gift?

---

[39] As Yeshua summed up this parable, he likened it to the time when He will return and divide the nations. In the similar parable in Luke, Yeshua ended it a little differently. Our application to this parable will stop after their explanation of the rewards as that is very applicable to this present analogy of the kingdom.

As servants of God, we absolutely have total choice on how we live our life. The things that God has given to us, that which we possess in the natural, we put it on the Altar, and we embrace the things that God has given us in the spiritual. As we combine the motivation of our being, *living for God and His kingdom*, with the power of the Holy Spirit living in us, we bring forth good fruit for God's kingdom. We double what we've been given!

When totally sold out to the things of God, totally yielded to His Spirit, choose to embrace Heaven's Challenge, and when our life is done, we'll hear those cherished and desired words: "well done thy good and faithful servant". We'll then step into our eternal reward.

PERSONAL REFLECTION
Dear Reader, this is a sobering chapter with so many powerful truths that challenge our entire being. Do not close out this chapter, please, without some serious time spent with YeHoVaH. It is far too important a topic to put off until another day!

HEAVEN'S MESSAGE EXPRESSED

"For I say unto you, That except your righteousness shall exceed the righteousness of the scribes and Pharisees, ye shall in no case enter into the kingdom of heaven."

Matthew 5:20

Thus far, we've looked outside the fence, *the area where heaven's picture,[40] prophetically shows the world.* Through the world, the place of man's present existence, we discover the entrance way to heaven, *the gate,* which after entering, includes living and walking in the kingdom of heaven with God, *in the here and now.* That aspect is clearly shown in the Tabernacle of Moses, *seen in the outer court, PRIOR* to entering the actual tabernacle. Prophetically speaking, this *outer court is an*

---

[40] The Tabernacle of Moses

extension of Heaven, and what is typically called the "kingdom of heaven" upon the earth.

As we walk with YeHoVaH, living out our life before His face, we do so *as an extension of God's kingdom*. Earth needs to know there is more than what meets humanity's natural (or even spiritual) eye. Since mankind must make decisions here that affect their eternal destiny, they need exposure to aspects of the kingdom's existence.

Therefore, God in His mercy, places a longing within each person to know the Creator[41]. Also, in numerous and varied ways, He lets mankind experience certain aspects of His kingdom on the earth. One dynamic way YeHoVaH does this is to introduce someone or something[42] about His kingdom into a person's life, helping them to explore the desire to know the creator. No one from His kingdom came with greater insight and impact than the only begotten Son of YeHoVaH. Yeshua's accurate teachings and manifestations of the kingdom of God give

---

[41] "Who will have all men to be saved, and to come unto the knowledge of the truth." (1 Timothy 2:4)

[42] It might be a problem requiring God's solution

clarity to understanding the hidden mysteries of heaven since He came from heaven!

> John 6:38
> 6 For I came down from heaven, not to do mine own will, but the will of him that sent me.

Prior to the days of Yeshua, YeHoVaH gave us the prophets to talk to us and teach us, as well as the external evidences of prophetic pictures, such as the Tabernacle of Moses and the Temple of Solomon, etc. Since the days of Yeshua's ascension into heaven, YeHoVaH continues to introduce people from His kingdom into our lives. These believers "born from above" have a responsibility to live out their life manifesting the things of the kingdom of God. As they live out their life, manifesting the true works of the Almighty, they bring the kingdom of God near for others to embrace:

Yeshua said;

> Matthew 12:28
> 28 But if I cast out devils by the Spirit of God, then the kingdom of God is come unto you.

Luke 10:8-11
> 8 And into whatsoever city ye enter, and they receive you, eat such things as are set before you: 9 And heal the sick that are therein, and say unto them, The kingdom of God is come nigh unto you. 10 But into whatsoever city ye enter, and they receive you not, go your ways out into the streets of the same, and say, 11 Even the very dust of your city, which cleaveth on us, we do wipe off against you: notwithstanding be ye sure of this, that the kingdom of God is come nigh unto you.

In these two scriptures, people experienced the kingdom of God near to them. In one case, devils were removed, (cast out), and in the other case, healing came to sick people. Onlookers, as well as those experiencing the mighty works, knew something happened. While not everyone will receive the explanation, nevertheless, Yeshua commanded His disciples to declare the kingdom of God came near.

God's kingdom *coming near* is not the same thing as that of *a person entering*. Therefore, a person can experience the influence of the kingdom of God, yet not be part of it. Later, in fact, they may even deny that anything happened, or can make excuses to attribute its effects to something totally different. Again, there are choices to be made as humankind encounters the kingdom of God!

Those mighty works done through the power of the Holy Spirit, however, manifest the reality of the kingdom of God. Disciples commanding this kind of power from the kingdom of God were expected to utilize it, and often. In addition, they were expected to give it freely:

> Matthew 10:7-8
> 7 And as ye go, preach, saying, The kingdom of heaven is at hand. 8 Heal the sick, cleanse the lepers, raise the dead, cast out devils: freely ye have received, freely give.

As true disciples of Yeshua, then and now, walk out their faith in power, they do so from their position inside the kingdom of God. What manifests in their lives results from their relationship with YeHoVaH, as they walk out their faith in obedience before Him in fear and trembling[43].

Genuine manifestations of such power are an extension of heaven, and this extension of heaven is seen prophetically, in many ways, within the Tabernacle of Moses. The Brazen Altar, as we saw in the last chapter, shows a willing death to self as one becomes a living sacrifice unto YeHoVaH. That means one follows His will in all things. To God, that is our reasonable service.

Further descriptions of the kingdom of heaven show up in the many duties of the priests, operating within the Tabernacle of Moses system. Of Levi, YeHoVaH said:

Malachi 2:4-7
> 4 And ye shall know that I have sent this commandment unto you, that my covenant might be with Levi, saith YeHoVaH of hosts. 5 My covenant was

---

[43] "Wherefore, my beloved, as ye have always obeyed, not as in my presence only, but now much more in my absence, work out your own salvation with fear and trembling." (Philippians 2:12)

with him of life and peace; and I gave them to him for the fear wherewith he feared me, and was afraid before my name. 6 The law of truth was in his mouth, and iniquity was not found in his lips: he walked with me in peace and equity, and did turn many away from iniquity. 7 For the priest's lips should keep knowledge, and they should seek the law at his mouth: for he is the messenger of YeHoVaH of hosts.

Attributes of priests, living under the first covenant, carries the prophetic picture well. So do the principles carried over to those in Messiah today:

- Fear of YeHoVaH
- Law of truth in his mouth,
- Iniquity not found in his lips
- Walked with YeHoVaH in peace and equity (uprightness)
- Turned many away from iniquity.
- The priest's lips kept knowledge
- People could see the Torah (Instructions of God) at his mouth
- He was the messenger of YeHoVaH Tseva'ot. (YeHoVaH of Hosts)

Priests of YeHoVaH spoke of the kingdom to teach and extend a helping hand to others so they, too, may enter the kingdom. They gave instructions from God's Word on personal behaviour regarding God's requirement to make that entrance possible. Some priests, (as noted in an earlier chapter,) did not properly execute their duties. Of this Yeshua spoke:

> Matthew 5:20
> 20 For I say unto you, That except your righteousness shall exceed the righteousness of the scribes and Pharisees, ye shall in no case enter into the kingdom of heaven.

And also:

> Matthew 23:13-15
> 13 ¶ But woe unto you, scribes and Pharisees, hypocrites! for ye shut up the kingdom of heaven against men: for ye neither go in yourselves, neither suffer ye them that are entering to go in. 14 Woe unto you, scribes and Pharisees, hypocrites! for ye devour widows' houses, and for a pretence make long prayer: therefore ye shall receive the greater

damnation. 15 Woe unto you, scribes and Pharisees, hypocrites! for ye compass sea and land to make one proselyte, and when he is made, ye make him twofold more the child of hell than yourselves.

In these two passages we see the failure of the religious system as it propagated those who obviously knew the scriptures, including the instructions and necessary behaviour to enter the kingdom of heaven, yet did not align their own behaviour with the requirements of YeHoVaH! They taught it to others, adding to them burdens of behaviour which they would not even consider doing themselves:

Matthew 23:2-4

> 2 Saying, The scribes and the Pharisees sit in Moses' seat: 3 All therefore whatsoever Moses[44] bid you observe, that observe and do; but do not ye after their works *(those of the Pharisees):* [45]for they say, and do not. 4 For they bind heavy burdens and grievous to be borne, and lay them on men's

---

[44]The word which KJV interpret as "they" (as is in original KJV) is masculine singular, referring to Moses, not "they" referring to the scribes and Pharisees.
[45] Italics added for clarity.

shoulders; but they themselves will not move them with one of their fingers.

Religious leaders, bound within the outward performance of a religious system, knew the way. They declared it with their lips, stating that one enters the kingdom of heaven, meek, humble and dependent upon God. Yet, they obeyed not the words of YeHoVaH. They were proud, boastful, arrogant and often voided the commandments of YeHoVaH. Yeshua spoke of their arrogance, and He spoke of a proper attitude for all to display, including kings, princes, elders, pharisees and priests:

Mark 10:13-16
> 13 And they brought young children to him, that he should touch them: and his disciples rebuked those that brought them. 14 But when Jesus saw it, he was much displeased, and said unto them, Suffer the little children to come unto me, and forbid them not: for of such is the kingdom of God. 15 Verily I say unto you, Whosoever shall not receive the kingdom of God as a little child, he shall not enter therein. 16 And he took them up in his arms, put his hands upon them, and blessed them.

Matthew 18:3-4
> 3 And said, Verily I say unto you, Except ye be converted, and become as little children, ye shall not enter into the kingdom of heaven. 4 Whosoever therefore shall humble himself as this little child, the same is greatest in the kingdom of heaven.

In our pursuit of understanding heaven, we must come face to face with the reality that religious leaders, their teachings and their behaviours might well be deceiving! Religion is not the answer! Only a relationship with God is the answer, and that relationship produces the good fruit of the kingdom.

Matthew 7:15-20
> 15 ¶ Beware of false prophets, which come to you in sheep's clothing, but inwardly they are ravening wolves. 16 Ye shall know them by their fruits. Do men gather grapes of thorns, or figs of thistles? 17 Even so every good tree bringeth forth good fruit; but a corrupt tree bringeth forth evil fruit. 18 A good tree cannot bring forth evil fruit, neither can a corrupt tree bring forth good

fruit. 19 Every tree that bringeth not forth good fruit is hewn down, and cast into the fire. 20 Wherefore by their fruits ye shall know them.

As we look at the fruit, we can compare it to the prophetic picture of heaven given in the scriptures. Do those ministers of the gospel follow in the type outlined by the prophetic picture? If so, those who claim to be of that kingdom act like that kingdom and they express heaven's message, wholeheartedly.

Certainly, there is room for error and improvements in even the most dedicated servant's behaviour, but the overall heart of the one born of God's Spirit moves with His heart, with His life and with His power. In other words, one from that kingdom looks very much like Yeshua!

PERSONAL REFLECTION:
Another sobering chapter, isn't it? Our life as a born-again citizen of heaven prophetically speaks of the kingdom of God, in the character of God we demonstrate. Accept the challenge, dear one, and go before YeHoVaH. Inquire of

Him and consider asking these very personal questions:

YeHoVaH:

- How am I doing in displaying the true aspects of the kingdom of God?
- Am I living like Yeshua, dedicated, faithful and true in every area of my life?
- Please show me, YeHoVaH, where I do well and where I fall short.

After you do that, know that He will respond. It might be immediately, or through some circumstance in your life, but do know that He will answer you!

Chapter 7 Heaven's Message Expressed

HEAVEN'S MAJESTIC REFLECTION

"Messiah, also loved the church, and gave himself for it; That he might sanctify and cleanse it with the washing of water by the word."

Ephesians 5:25c-26

Before we leave the outside perimeters, that which is housed inside the gate, we need to stop at the Laver. This was a bronze basin made from the mirrors of the women and brimming with water. It was placed before the entrance to the tabernacle as an easy access for the priests, prior to the entry into the Holy Place. As the priest used the water in this Laver made of mirrors to wash, his reflection would easily been seen, *prior to* his entrance into the tabernacle. Now, the washing of the hands and feet of the priest had its practical purpose, but we wish to look at its prophetic picture!

Primarily, the prophetic picture comes clear as we look at the reflective properties of the Laver. What did the Laver reflect? In its actual physical properties, it reflected the one who peered into it. Prophetically, it shows us a majestic reflection of a very important thing. James, the Apostle, refers to that in his writings:

> James 1:22-24
> 22 But be ye doers of the word, and not hearers only, deceiving your own selves. 23 For if any be a hearer of the word, and not a doer, he is like unto a man beholding his natural face in a glass: (a mirror) 24 For he beholdeth himself, and goeth his way, and straightway forgetteth what manner of man he was.

James compares the Word to a mirror. A person looks in the mirror of the Word, and by understanding the Word, sees his/her reflection. God's Word, therefore, is like a mirror reflecting what man ought to be! Man, created in God's image, should greatly resemble the Creator! One human being, close to the Father's heart, did! His name was Yeshua. Yeshua, the Word of God, mirrored God's creation perfectly.

John 1:1-4, 14

> 1 In the beginning was the Word, and the Word was with God, and the Word was God. 2 The same was in the beginning with God. 3 All things were made by him; and without him was not any thing made that was made. 4 In him was life; and the life was the light of men."
>
> 14 And the Word was made flesh, and dwelt among us, (and we beheld his glory, the glory as of the only begotten of the Father,) full of grace and truth.

Clearly, to see Yeshua, is to see the Father:

John 14:9-11

> 9 Jesus saith unto him, Have I been so long time with you, and yet hast thou not known me, Philip? he that hath seen me hath seen the Father; and how sayest thou then, Shew us the Father? 10 Believest thou not that I am in the Father, and the Father in me? the words that I speak unto you I speak not of myself: but the Father

that dwelleth in me, he doeth the works.
11 Believe me that I am in the Father, and
the Father in me: or else believe me for the
very works' sake.

Yeshua, clearly and without any compromise or worldly adaptation, portrayed the Father. He did so in all circumstances. Thus, in the final moments Yeshua spent with His disciples before the cross, He could confidently declare that He and His Father were one!

Yeshua came, as did the prophets of old, to call mankind to repentance and to make that road back to YeHoVaH incredibly clear. He did not come to brand that road as easy, but rather, to point out its accessibility to all who desired to enter the kingdom. Those who choose to enter have a responsibility to remember the oneness of the Father with the Son, and the Son with the Father, but in addition, the oneness of believers with Yeshua. Yeshua spoke of that oneness:

John 17:11-26

11 ¶ And now I am no more in the world,
but these are in the world, and I come to
thee. Holy Father keep through thine own
name those whom thou hast given me, that

they may be one, as we [are]. 12 While I was with them in the world, I kept them in thy name: those that thou gavest me I have kept, and none of them is lost, but the son of perdition; that the scripture might be fulfilled. 13 And now come I to thee; and these things I speak in the world, that they might have my joy fulfilled in themselves. 14 I have given them thy word; and the world hath hated them, because they are not of the world, even as I am not of the world. 15 I pray not that thou shouldest take them out of the world, but that thou shouldest keep them from the evil. 16 They are not of the world, even as I am not of the world."

"17 ¶ Sanctify them through thy truth: thy word is truth. 18 As thou hast sent me into the world, even so have I also sent them into the world. 19 And for their sakes I sanctify myself, that they also might be sanctified through the truth."

"20 ¶ Neither pray I for these alone, but for them also which shall believe on me through their word; 21 That they all may be one; as thou, Father, [art] in me, and I in thee, that they also may be one in us: that the world may believe that thou hast sent

> me. 22 And the glory which thou gavest me I have given them; that they may be one, even as we are one: 23 I in them, and thou in me, that they may be made perfect in one; and that the world may know that thou hast sent me, and hast loved them, as thou hast loved me."
>
> "24 ¶ Father, I will that they also, whom thou hast given me, be with me where I am; that they may behold my glory, which thou hast given me: for thou lovedst me before the foundation of the world. 25 O righteous Father, the world hath not known thee: but I have known thee, and these have known that thou hast sent me. 26 And I have declared unto them thy name and will declare [it]: that the love wherewith thou hast loved me may be in them, and I in them."

After the cross, a further understanding of that oneness is seen in the writings of the Apostle, Paul:

> Ephesians 2:4-10
>
> 4 But God, who is rich in mercy, for his great love wherewith he loved us, 5 Even when we were dead in sins, hath quickened

us together with Christ, (by grace ye are saved;) 6 And hath raised [us] up together, and made [us] sit together in heavenly [places] in Christ Jesus: 7 That in the ages to come he might shew the exceeding riches of his grace in [his] kindness toward us through Christ Jesus. 8 For by grace are ye saved through faith; and that not of yourselves: [it is] the gift of God: 9 Not of works, lest any man should boast. 10 For we are his workmanship, created in Christ Jesus unto good works, which God hath before ordained that we should walk in them."

That oneness we have in Messiah is so very important! As we embrace it, it brings connectivity which results in unity of thought and purpose. There is no other way in which we can live out our Christian lives and make the impact YeHoVaH desires. We must do it out of our place of oneness in Messiah[46]. As we walk that out, we walk in the Spirit, then like Yeshua, we too should reveal the beauty and character of our Master and Lord!

---

[46] We'll look more at that oneness as we enter Section 3 and look at the Throne Room of the Almighty.

To look at believers, today, is a good part of YeHoVaH's plan to show His character, however, the written Word of God has attributes that are timeless and always applicable. That Word should always be the focus of anyone searching for God. It is, THE MIRROR, where we truly see ourselves! With God's Word, we see areas of praise, where God's work has accomplished much, and we see areas which still need the excavating work of the Holy Spirit. The Word of God gives us the reality check we need to live our life pleasing to the Almighty!

In referring to the Word and its importance, Yeshua taught a parable.

Matthew 13:3-9
> 3 And he spake many things unto them in parables, saying, Behold, a sower went forth to sow; 4 And when he sowed, some [seeds] fell by the way side, and the fowls came and devoured them up: 5 Some fell upon stony places, where they had not much earth: and forthwith they sprung up, because they had no deepness of earth: 6 And when the sun was up, they were scorched; and because they had no root, they withered away. 7 And some fell

among thorns; and the thorns sprung up, and choked them: 8 But other fell into good ground, and brought forth fruit, some an hundredfold, some sixtyfold, some thirtyfold. 9 Who hath ears to hear, let him hear.

While this parable has managed to puzzle a few people, Yeshua explained the parable, and so from His explanation, we attain its meaning.

Prior to reading the interpretation, keep in mind that there is a direct correlation between the heart, which is the place of thought, and the Word of God. The condition of the heart is incredibly important. That is clear by the words Yeshua spoke, just prior to clarifying the parable's meaning:

Matthew 13:11-17

11 He answered and said unto them, Because it is given unto you to know the mysteries of the kingdom of heaven, but to them it is not given. 12 For whosoever hath, to him shall be given, and he shall have more abundance: but whosoever hath not, from him shall be taken away even that he hath. 13 Therefore speak I to them in parables: because they seeing see not; and

hearing they hear not, neither do they understand. 14 And in them is fulfilled the prophecy of Esaias, which saith, By hearing ye shall hear, and shall not understand; and seeing ye shall see, and shall not perceive: 15 For this people's heart is waxed gross, and [their] ears are dull of hearing, and their eyes they have closed; lest at any time they should see with [their] eyes, and hear with [their] ears, and should understand with [their] heart, and should be converted, and I should heal them. 16 But blessed [are] your eyes, for they see: and your ears, for they hear. 17 For verily I say unto you, That many prophets and righteous [men] have desired to see [those things] which ye see, and have not seen [them]; and to hear [those things] which ye hear, and have not heard [them].

One who seeks the truth, who truly desires the things of YeHoVaH to manifest in their own life, including a brokenness to manifest His amazing divine nature to others, has a heart prepared for receiving!

Matthew 13:18-23

18 Hear ye therefore the parable of the sower. 19 When any one heareth the word

of the kingdom, and understandeth it not, then cometh the wicked one, and catcheth away that which was sown in his heart. This is he which received seed by the way side.

20 But he that received the seed into stony places, the same is he that heareth the word, and anon with joy receiveth it; 21 Yet hath he not root in himself, but dureth for a while: for when tribulation or persecution ariseth because of the word, by and by he is offended. 22 He also that received seed among the thorns is he that heareth the word; and the care of this world, and the deceitfulness of riches, choke the word, and he becometh unfruitful. 23 But he that received seed into the good ground is he that heareth the word, and understandeth it; which also beareth fruit, and bringeth forth, some an hundredfold, some sixty, some thirty.

Yeshua clarified the fact that the "seed" is the Word of God. Let's see how it's received in the hearts of the listeners:

- When anyone hears the word of the kingdom, and *they don't understand it*, they, obviously, can't embrace that word.

Then, as it is loosely held by them, the wicked one, (ha satan) comes and snatches the word away. With the seed stolen, it cannot take root and bring forth fruit.
- Next person shows the seed (the Word) falling on stony ground. This person heard the word and received it with joy. Then, tribulation or persecution came because of the word they received. Being offended, they let it go. Again, the word bears no fruit.
- Next the seed fell among thorns. This person hears the word but the cares of the world, the deceitfulness of the things of the world, such as riches, gets the attention. Such things as fear of man, or a self-focused desire to succeed in life with one's own plans take over the person's goals in their heart. They begin to live for other things. The seed (the word) which was to produce fruit, does not do so.
- The next person of whom Yeshua spoke received the word and understood it. He made it his life's commitment. Consequently, it brought forth fruit in

varying degrees, according to the person's ability and calling.[47]

As a person allows the Word of God to penetrate their heart, as they allow it to change their mindsets, values and desires, they stay within the Word. A one-time reading is not enough! They embrace the Word, loving its very message, devoting their heart to understanding and living out what YeHoVaH desires of them.

For these people, the ones who embrace the Word of God and allow it to bring forth fruit, they begin to emulate Heaven's Majestic Reflection of the one who created them and gave them this new life in Messiah. Certainly, their lives, in words and deeds, point to the only one who is the perfect image of YeHoVaH, which is our Yeshua.

PERSONAL REFLECTION

As a person lives their life before YeHoVaH, things will arrive at their doorstep and knock softly, or hard at their door. Some of those arrivals at a believer's door may have a loud

---

[47] At least, this is the author's understanding of why some produce 100, 60 and 30.

voice, or perhaps a soft and gentle voice that says, "Come, follow me". This might be the voice of popularity, or a simple, harmless-looking distraction purposed to pull its victim off target. Those who are in the Word of God, those who know the principles of the Word and the basic content of it, hopefully, recognize the deceiver's voice and say "No, it does not fit in with my life's goals to be like Yeshua!"

How are you at discerning "voices" speaking to you regarding life's direction. Whether those voices are loud or soft, what calls out to you? Ask the Father to open your ears to things that knock on your door, and to help you recognize what is not from His kingdom. Ask YeHoVaH to help you discern if you truly grasp the way in which you're presently headed. Ask Him to help you lay out before Him what you presently know about your destiny and if any changes may be needed in order to follow His Plans to attain that God-ordained destiny.[48] Ask YeHoVaH how much you look like Yeshua and if you represent Him well!

---

[48] Perhaps these scriptures may help you: John 10:1-5, John 10:14

SECTION 3: INSIDE THE HOLY PLACE

THE PRIESTHOOD:
Receive it
THE FIVE PILLARS & VEIL:
Utilize it
THE TABLE OF SHEWBREAD:
Partake of it
THE MENORAH:
Enlightened by it
THE ALTAR OF INCENSE:
Offer prayers upon it

HEAVEN'S PECULIAR TREASURE

"Now therefore, if ye will obey my voice indeed, and keep my covenant, then ye shall be a peculiar treasure unto me above all people: for all the earth [is] mine".

Exodus 19:5

Thus far in this study, we've looked at a gradual path to the tabernacle, beginning at the entrance, (the gate), moving past the brazen Altar, and then the bronze Laver. At this point, our next stop would be the entrance to the Holy Place. Prior to entering, however, we're going to do a little back tracking, to the time prior to the revelation of the Tabernacle of Moses. Doing this brings a powerful focus on an amazing plan which YeHoVaH set in place, which we might otherwise overlook. In addition, it sets a foundation for greater insight as we enter the tabernacle, beginning at the Holy Place.

A LOOK BACK:

Once the Almighty carried the children of Israel out of Egypt on eagle's wings and brought them to the base of Mount Sinai, He made a covenant with them.

Exodus 19:4-8

> "Ye have seen what I did unto the Egyptians, and *how* I bare you on eagles' wings, and brought you unto myself. Now therefore, if ye will obey my voice indeed, and keep my covenant, then ye shall be a peculiar treasure unto me above all people: for all the earth *is* mine: And ye shall be unto me a kingdom of priests, and an holy nation. These *are* the words which thou shalt speak unto the children of Israel. And Moses came and called for the elders of the people, and laid before their faces all these words which the LORD commanded him. And all the people answered together, and said, All that the LORD hath spoken we will do. And Moses returned the words of the people unto the LORD."

This covenant had clear parameters, with God's promise clearly stated, as well as the desired obligation from His People. YeHoVaH commanded the people to obey His voice and keep His Covenant. In doing this, becoming a kingdom of priests before YeHoVaH's face, behaving exactly as YeHoVaH prescribed, these people were destined as a prized possession of YeHoVaH.

This clear, specific, and intentional destiny came with deliberate choices of the redeemed individuals from slavery in Egypt. Each was to walk in the ways of YeHoVaH, namely obeying His Voice and doing His commands. Each person would minister to YeHoVaH, as YeHoVaH required and their behaviour, always, would reflect His desires.

In summary, these redeemed individuals would live holy lives before YeHoVaH. As a kingdom of priests, they would be a holy nation, serving the Almighty, reflecting His ways to all who looked on. Consequently, their lives, in contrast to other nations around them, would stand out as unique. Their behaviour, goals and purpose for living, for all intents and purposes, YeHoVaH designed as distinctly different from other nations around them who knew not YeHoVaH, as Israel knew Him. That uniqueness would draw other nations to know the true God and be redeemed also. Israel agreed to these terms. [49]

A VISITATION FROM HEAVEN

After the people agreed to the terms of the covenant, they prepared to meet YeHoVaH, as He promised to come down to them.

Exodus 19:9-13

> 9 ¶ And YeHoVaH said unto Moses, Lo, I come unto thee in a thick cloud, that the people may hear when I speak with thee, and believe thee for ever. And Moses told the words of the people unto YeHoVaH. 10 And YeHoVaH said unto Moses, Go unto the people, and sanctify them to day and to morrow, and let them wash their clothes, 11 And be ready against the third day: for the third day YeHoVaH will come down in the sight of all the people upon mount Sinai. 12 And thou shalt set bounds unto the people round about, saying, Take heed to yourselves, that ye go not up into the mount, or touch the border of it: whosoever

---

[49] Exodus 19: 7-8

toucheth the mount shall be surely put to death: 13 There shall not an hand touch it, but he shall surely be stoned, or shot through; whether it be beast or man, it shall not live: when the trumpet soundeth long, they shall come up to the mount.

With safety measures in place, the people stood around the mountain. YeHoVaH descended. He spoke to them out of the cloud:

Exodus 19:16-20

> 16 And it came to pass on the third day in the morning, that there were thunders and lightnings, and a thick cloud upon the mount, and the voice of the trumpet exceeding loud; so that all the people that was in the camp trembled.
>
> 17 And Moses brought forth the people out of the camp to meet with God; and they stood at the nether part of the mount. 18 And mount Sinai was altogether on a smoke, because YeHoVaH descended upon it in fire: and the smoke thereof ascended as the smoke of a furnace, and the whole mount quaked greatly.

19 And when the voice of the trumpet sounded long, and waxed louder and louder, Moses spake, and God answered him by a voice. 20 And YeHoVaH came down upon mount Sinai, on the top of the mount: and YeHoVaH called Moses up to the top of the mount; and Moses went up.

This visitation, *which was a precursor to God dwelling in their midst*, provides an amazing scene of God upon the mountain. Here, God spoke His commandments. [50] Yet, the people could not bear to hear the Words of YeHoVaH, directly from His mouth. They responded, however with a commitment to do whatsoever Moses revealed to them.

Exodus 20:19

19 And they said unto Moses, Speak thou with us, and we will hear: but let not God speak with us, lest we die.

Exodus 24:3

3 And Moses came and told the people all the words of YeHoVaH, and all the judgments: and all the people answered

---

[50]Exodus 20:1-17

with one voice, and said, All the words which YeHoVaH hath said will we do.

Moses, shortly thereafter, makes a blood sacrifice, inaugurating that covenant.

Exodus 24:7-8

> 7 And he took the book of the covenant, and read in the audience of the people: and they said, All that YeHoVaH hath said will we do, and be obedient.
>
> 8 And Moses took the blood, and sprinkled it on the people, and said, Behold the blood of the covenant, which YeHoVaH hath made with you concerning all these words.

This, therefore, is the blood covenant YeHoVaH made with Israel, who committed with their own words, to obey the voice of the Almighty. Shortly thereafter, Moses ascends the mount with YeHoVaH, and in his absence, the people break this covenant with YeHoVaH.

A further reading of this scripture shows YeHoVaH as forgiving and moving in a secondary plan. He wanted to live in their midst, however, once the covenant was broken, He gave Moses a plan to erect a tabernacle, with specific instructions to copy heaven's, as he saw it on the mount.

Later, YeHoVaH's glory cloud appeared, after they built the tabernacle, showing the Almighty dwelling in their midst.

PROPHETIC PICTURE AND REALITIES

In this brief summary of scripture, we see God's desire to redeem a people and bring them unto Himself. In summary we see:

- God carried them out of Egypt on eagle's wings
- He brought to Himself, a people redeemed
- God came in a thick cloud upon a mountain
- God spoke with them
- God invited them to obey Him
- God promised rewards for their behaviour
- He called the people to live holy lives
- He called the people to embrace a royal priesthood. [51]

---

[51] God gave them a different priesthood, namely, the Aaronic priesthood.

- He gave the people an outlined behaviour, which they drastically failed to comply

Prophetically, as YeHoVaH came down upon the mountain, we see a powerful comparison to the visitation of YeHoVaH, in the person of Yeshua.

- God came to earth[52], in the person of Yeshua
- Through Yeshua, YeHoVaH redeemed mankind
- After Yeshua's ascension, YeHoVaH sent the Holy Spirit
- The Holy Spirit dwelt within believers, cleansed by the blood of the Lamb
- YeHoVaH gave a prescribed form of behaviour to live holy before His Face
- YeHoVaH gave a priesthood for all believers to follow, that of Melchizadek, the same as Yeshua.

This prophetic parallel of the first covenant to the second, must be kept in mind as we proceed further into the understanding of Heaven, as

---

[52] Isaiah 7:14 Therefore YeHoVaH himself shall give you a sign; Behold, a virgin shall conceive, and bear a son, and shall call his name Immanuel.

believers are positioned in heavenly places and are invited to function in their priesthood. The failure of Israel to comply in being a kingdom of priests, necessitated the giving of the Aaronic priesthood. That priesthood shifted later to the greater order of Melchizadek, as the Aaronic became obsolete. However, God's invitation to His people must be noted. God desires all His people to be priests unto Him. In Yeshua, believers are kings and priests unto God, in the order of Melchizadek.[53]

When God's people live within their invited position, they become God's treasured possession.[54] This is because, when totally sold out to YeHoVaH, believers listen to their Heavenly Father's voice, and obey! As believers in Messiah, let us never forget that as we walk out our priesthood before YeHoVaH, we are a treasured possession, one He holds dear in His Hand!

---

[53] 1st order of priesthood was Adamic. Next was Aaronic, next was Melchizadek. If you wish to learn more, why not consider a study of this author, entitled, Arising Incense.

[54] Exodus 19:5 Now therefore, if ye will obey my voice indeed, and keep my covenant, then ye shall be a peculiar treasure unto me above all people: for all the earth is mine:

PERSONAL REFLECTION

As one explains a spiritual truth, it often means challenges for a teacher to clearly express and for listens to wholly embrace. So, at this chapter's end, to facilitate learning, instead of a personal reflection, let us take time to ensure reader and author are on the same page regarding the prophetic picture of the Tabernacle of Moses. Please review the diagrams and comments on the next two pages, before starting the next chapter.

LIFE OUTSIDE THE KINGDOM:

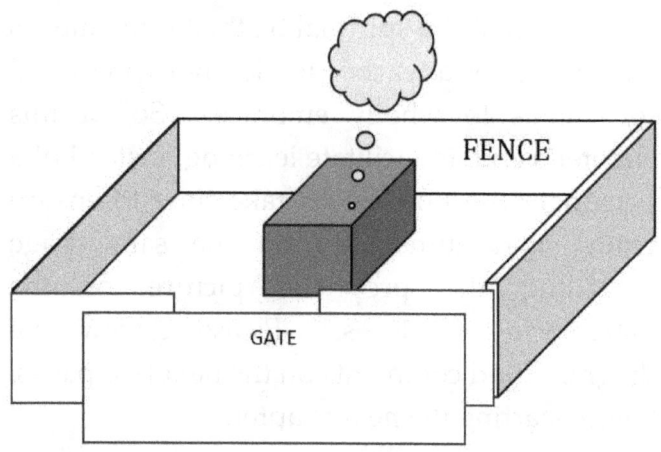

1. People do not see the kingdom of YeHoVaH
2. People only see the effects of the kingdom of God, enough to know it exists
3. YeHoVaH invites humankind to enter the kingdom *during* their lifetime upon this earth
4. Should a person accept the invitation, the kingdom of God moves within them, and from their position in Messiah, they function
5. These people now live their life in the "Spirit"

LIFE WITHIN THE KINGDOM
(IN THE SPIRIT)

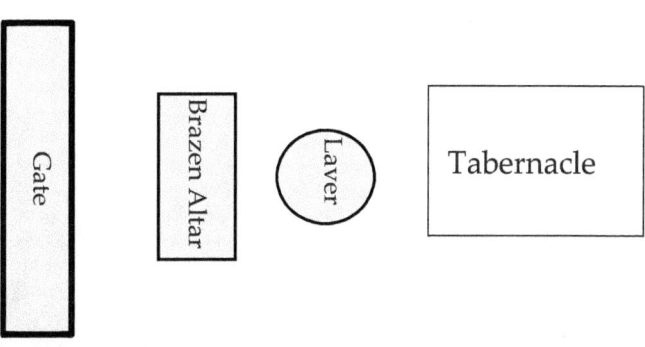

1. As a part of the kingdom of YeHoVaH, believers become a "living sacrifice" unto God.
2. Believers live submitted to YeHoVaH, in every aspect.
3. Believers function as a priest (after the order of Melchizadek) unto the Almighty.
4. Believers sit in heavenly places in Messiah[55]

---

[55] Discussed at the end of the next chapter

HEAVEN'S UNSHAKEABLE GOVERNMENT[56]

"YeHoVaH hath prepared his throne in the heavens; and his kingdom ruleth overall. Bless YeHoVaH, ye his angels, that excel in strength, that do his commandments, hearkening unto the voice of his word. Bless ye YeHoVaH, all [ye] his hosts; [ye] ministers of his, that do his pleasure."

Psalm 103:19-21

In the above scripture passage, we catch a glimpse of the extent of the government of the Almighty, that government here being

---

[56] This chapter gives a few highlights of God's government. If you wish to learn more about this topic, consider the book, "Heaven's Greater Government". It goes into much greater detail on how God's Government functions in our world. See Appendix under "Other Books by this Author".

alluded to by David, the author of this passage. David uses the term, throne, which represents the centre of authority within a kingdom. In speaking of the throne of YeHoVaH, David clearly tells us that "YeHoVaH's throne is firmly established (prepared) in the heavens, and the extent of His governmental rule is over all"[57].

David further expresses his understanding of the government of YeHoVaH, remarking that "His angels excel in strength and do His commandments, for certainly, they listen to His voice". Additionally, David comments, "all YeHoVaH's hosts", which are heavenly armies, fulfil YeHoVaH's will, as do the faithful servants of YeHoVaH.

In these three verses, we see that:
- **YeHoVaH has a throne:** *(vs 19)*
  - That throne is firmly fixed
  - It cannot be moved and certainly, never removed

- **YeHoVaH operates with governmental authority:** *(vs 19)*
  - YeHoVaH's government centres around Him. (In earthly terms, we

---
[57] KJV paraphrased by author

call this form of government theocratic.)

- YeHoVaH's government, like His throne, is firmly established, and therefore, can neither be shaken nor removed.

- **YeHoVaH's government is over all:** (*vs 19)*
    - There is no limit to this government's right to rule, jurisdiction, or effectiveness.
    - This government is limitless in scope, operation & effectiveness.

- **YeHoVaH has regulations & commands and clearly communicates them:** *(vs 20)*
    - Angelic emissaries, who are valiant, mighty and strong, hear YeHoVaH's voice and obey His commands.
    - Clear communication flows from the headship of YeHoVaH's government to those who live and function under Him, for they hear His voice. They follow the rules and regulations in YeHoVaH's kingdom.

- **YeHoVaH's will is done[58]:** *(vs 21)*
  - Armies and YeHoVaH's servants fulfil His will (do His pleasure).
  - Heaven's administrative staff, along with those who fall into the category of servant on this earth, are loyal to Him as they do His will, do His pleasure.

In these few verses of scripture, we see some evidence to strongly affirm that, without a doubt, YeHoVaH has an operative and functioning kingdom. As such, its extent and scope are limitless, and thus, very difficult for our finite minds to embrace. Therefore, this aspect of the kingdom of YeHoVaH is also seen within the tabernacle of Moses.

This structure of Moses, as we saw earlier, had a tented building, called the Tabernacle. Inside the tabernacle were two chambers, however, that division was not visible from the outside. To pass into that tented building, then, one entered the first chamber, accessing it from the outer compound. One must enter in the prescribed fashion, or defined order laid out before them. Walking forward, then, from that

---

[58] His will is done in heaven and on earth. (Daniel 4:17;25)

outer compound into the tabernacle's first chamber, meant passing by five tall bronze pillars which stood stately and ominously at the tabernacle's entrance.

These five pillars held a massive veil, which concealed what rested inside. This concealing veil, the five pillars, along with the tall, gold covered walls, held the roof and side covering in place, thus, concealing the entire tabernacle to the eyes of those looking in from outside. Without that veil and covering, what's inside would be completely exposed or vulnerable. Only a specific order of entrance, with specific instructions as to preparation, made it possible for one to enter and thus know, first-hand, what exactly was kept inside.

Prophetically, this speaks a clear message on how to access God. To sum it up in one simple, power-packed statement, *we do it His Way!* God's established order or government over His kingdom, with its rules and regulations, must be obeyed, or there is no way in!

Access refused, man's ways,
Access approved, God's way!

Scripture portrays this fact. Prophetically, it is also seen in the entire layout of the Tabernacle of Moses, as it meticulously described the approach to God's throne (Holy of Holies). Lack of compliance meant death. So, as we approach the tabernacle's towering entrance, as we look up to the height of those five tall, stately pillars holding that massive veil, we see a portrayal of YeHoVaH's government.

Biblical scholars, who portray the Tabernacle of Moses as representing the church of Messiah, (the Ecclesia), often depict those five pillars as representative of the five-fold ministry of the church. In other words, the administration or government of the church, namely the apostle, prophet, pastor, teacher, and evangelist, are seen in the five bronze pillars, with the veil representing the body of believers.

Indeed, every church has its administrative structure, as does the individual family[59]. Without government in families, cities, principalities, provinces, territories or nations, there is no order, no *unity* of purpose, no means of obtaining a joint desired end. Governments provide the parameters whereby individuals govern their own choices. Governments

---

[59] The Father is the administrative head of the home.

provide helps, therefore, as well as deterrents to reach a desired end.

Without government in place, chaos arises. Without government, unruly behaviours manifest. Without government, there is no direction for a group of individuals to corporately lead. If one is to align people together, in any fashion, governments are mandatory.

It should be of no surprise, then, that YeHoVaH has a government and displays it, within the Tabernacle of Moses. When looking at the Tabernacle of Moses, in alignment with the Hebraic scriptures, we know all things point to YeHoshua:[60]

> Hebrews 10:7
> 7 Then said I, Lo, I come (in the volume of the book it is written of me,) to do thy will, O God.

This verse clearly states that the scriptures (volume of the book written of me) speaks of Yeshua. He is the primary interpretation of all

---

[60] Yehoshua is the long form for Yeshua, just as James is the long form for Jim. In Hebrew, please note, that the Father's name is in Him! To see Yeshua is to see the Father!

scripture, including prophetic pictures! Keeping that in mind, is Yeshua seen in the scriptures regarding heaven's government?

Hebrews 8:1-2

> 1 Now of the things which we have spoken this is the sum: We have such an high priest, who is set on the right hand of the throne of the Majesty in the heavens; 2 A minister of the sanctuary, and of the true tabernacle, which YeHoVaH pitched, and not man.

Here we see that Yeshua, in heaven, sits at the right hand of the throne of the Majesty in the heavens. This is a definite form of government, a sure and positive place of authority, wherein the Redeemer resides.

1 Peter 3:22 speaking of Yeshua:
> 22 Who is gone into heaven and is on the right hand of God; angels and authorities and powers being made subject unto him.

Here we see that angels and authorities and powers are made subject to Yeshua. These few scriptures, plus others[61], show us that Yeshua sits at God's right hand and therefore rules and

---

[61] Mark 12:36; Mark 16:19, Luke 22:69 to name a few

reigns, an active, emphatic, and definite part of heaven's government.

Heavens' government is unshakeable. It is not up for grabs! It is established and kept that way! God's word is final!

Psalm 119:89

> 89 For ever, O LORD, thy word is settled in heaven.

Yeshua, who sits at God's right hand, does so on behalf of all mankind. In love, and in order, to those who are born of His Spirit, He extends His awesome rulership, His authority for utilization on the earth:

Ephesians 2:4-7

> 4 But God, who is rich in mercy, for his great love wherewith he loved us, 5 Even when we were dead in sins, hath quickened us together with Christ, (by grace ye are saved;) 6 And hath raised us up together, and made us sit together in heavenly places in Christ Jesus: 7 That in the ages to come he might shew the exceeding riches of his grace in his kindness toward us through Christ Jesus.

This rulership overflows then, to those who walk in the kingdom of God, here upon the earth. It flows, not from a delegated authority given to believers, but from an authority resulting from our position in Messiah. In other words, our authority in Messiah is positional and it comes directly from the Throne Room of heaven. As we live out our lives, fulfilling the will of YeHoVaH, we utilize that positional authority to work with heaven to accomplish the tasks of the kingdom of God, upon the earth.

Such is the mercy and blessings of the Almighty, who redeemed us! Such is the victory of the only begotten Son of God, who came to earth that we might live eternally.

PERSONAL REFLECTION:

As you read this chapter reflecting upon the government of God, why not consider taking some time and investigate more scriptures that describe the government of the Almighty. It is truly awesome to study this aspect of the scriptures!

Regarding your position in Messiah, why not come before YeHoVaH, in prayer, and ask: "Do I operate within the positional authority of Yeshua? Show me where I do well and show me where I fall short!"

HEAVEN'S PERFECT PROVIDER

"But seek ye first the kingdom of God, and his righteousness; and all these things shall be added unto you."

Matthew 6:33

Throughout the tabernacle layout, we've seen a progression, moving from the outside gate to enter the tabernacle area, then we progress towards the Throne Room. YeHoVaH designed this progression to show there are certain specifics which need to be met before entering His Presence. If entering the presence of an earthly king has certain necessities, does one just waltz into the presence of the King of all the earth?

Access to YeHoVaH, as we've shown earlier, comes only through the gate, which prophetically typified Yeshua. Access via the first gate begins the relationship, but as in all relationships, intimacy grows with time spent together. In order to have a more intimate access with YeHoVaH, one must spend time with Him. To do this, again there are specifications, namely, one must utilize their priesthood.[62]

It is the Melchizedekian priesthood by which believers operate. This is a royal priesthood which comes from the believer's position in Messiah. As believers operate in this priesthood, it is imperative to understand what God made available to them.

This chapter begins a study of the Holy Place, and God's provision for us. Before going in that direction, however, let's ensure, one more time, we're on the same page.

A BELIEVER'S INVOLVEMENT IN HEAVEN

Most people believe heaven is somewhere they'll go after they die. However, believers need to understand their present life with its current involvement in heaven. In speaking on this subject, Paul, the Apostle, put it this way:

---

[62] We investigated this aspect in the chapter entitled, "Heaven's Promised Priesthood".

Ephesians 1:3

> Blessed be the God and Father of our Lord Jesus Christ, who hath blessed us with all spiritual blessings in heavenly places in Christ:

It is clear from this comment of the Apostle, Paul, that believers receive "all spiritual blessings" in heavenly places. First, this shows YeHoVaH lavishly poured out abundant blessings upon those in Messiah, forgetting nothing. There is no more YeHoVaH could give us. Second, we know all blessings that come to us have a place of origin. That place of origin is in "heavenly places".

HEAVENLY PLACES:

Believers have an intricate connection with the realm of heavenly places. Defining that realm, or heavenly places, is simple once you understand that the Tabernacle in the wilderness is a copy of the true tabernacle in heaven. In other words, to understand the term "heavenly places", we need to see it within its setting, namely, the true copy in heaven.

Believers, ones truly born of the Holy Spirit of YeHoVaH, intricately connect with heaven in that while still living in the flesh upon the earth, they are, nevertheless, positioned in the heavenly realm. This is so because true believers exist within Yeshua, Who lives in heavenly places:

Ephesians 1:19-23

> 19 And what is the exceeding greatness of his power to us-ward who believe, according to the working of his mighty power, 20 Which he wrought in Christ, when he raised him from the dead, and set him at his own right hand in the heavenly places, 21 Far above all principality, and power, and might, and dominion, and every name that is named, not only in this world, but also in that which is to come: 22 And hath put all things under his feet, and gave him to be the head over all things to the church, 23 Which is his body, the fulness of him that filleth all in all.

Yeshua, in accordance with scripture, rose from the dead, and is now seated at the right hand of YeHoVaH in heavenly places. By virtue of that position, He sits far above all things, including every name named, not only in this world, (those operative here on the earth, while it is in existence) but also in the world that is to come.

All things are put beneath His feet. He is given as the head over all things to the church (those in Him), for these are His body, the fulness of Him which fills all things.

Yeshua, in other words, is in heaven. From heaven, He sits above all things, principalities, power, might and dominion. His position, secure and immovable, puts Him in a place of authority or rule, like no other person. It is from there, He rules, waiting until His enemies become His footstool.

Knowing that is an amazing truth, but there is a truth even yet more amazing, which further details true believers' intricate connection with heaven, one in which we lightly touched upon, earlier:

Ephesians 2:4-7

> 4 But God, who is rich in mercy, for his great love wherewith he loved us, 5 Even when we were dead in sins, hath quickened us together with Christ, (by grace ye are saved;) 6 **And hath raised us up together, and made us sit together in heavenly places in Christ Jesus**: 7 That in the ages to come he might shew the exceeding riches of his

grace in his kindness toward us through Christ Jesus.

In case you didn't quite catch it, please read this again, *"And hath raised us up together, and made us sit together in heavenly places in Christ Jesus:"*.[63]

To make this clear, dear reader, if you are truly born of YeHoVaH's (YeHoshua's) Spirit, you are seated in heavenly places. This does *not mean* you *only have access* to heaven! It means far more! As genuine believers, we need to understand, this means we are positioned in heaven. Loosely put, this means believers "live" in heaven.

Of course, it is not that actual flesh and blood you that lives in heaven! It is the "Spirit" within you that resides there. However, it is from that place you're expected to minister to YeHoVaH, through your priesthood. It is from that place you are expected to receive from YeHoVaH. It is from that place you are expected to rest in the finished works of Yeshua. It is from that place, in Messiah, YeHoVaH expects you to do the good works foreordained for you to do!

---

[63] Ephesians 2:6

Ephesians 2:8-10

> 8 For by grace are ye saved through faith; and that not of yourselves: it is the gift of God: 9 Not of works, lest any man should boast. 10 For we are his workmanship, created in Christ Jesus unto good works, which God hath before ordained that we should walk in them.

As each true believer walks out their life upon this earth, the Holy Spirit resides within, thus giving them access to all they need, including the prized possession of heaven itself: *YeHoVaH, our Heavenly Father*.

Ephesians 2:18-22

> 18 For through him[64] we both have access by one Spirit unto the Father. 19 Now therefore ye are no more strangers and foreigners, but fellowcitizens with the saints, and of the household of God; 20 And are built upon the foundation of the apostles and prophets, Jesus Christ himself being the chief corner stone; 21 In whom all the building fitly framed together groweth unto an holy temple in

---

[64] Yeshua

YeHoVaH: 22 In whom ye also are builded together for an habitation of God through the Spirit.

We are in Him, and He is in us! We are His temple upon the earth, where He dwells within. Yet, by the power of the Holy Spirit, we live in heavenly places in Messiah, giving us more than just access to heaven! We have that access plus every provision we'll need! It all comes to us, by means of "all blessings in heavenly places".

In thinking of heavenly provisions and the provisional code of heaven, we must learn that everything we need is ready and waiting for us. The only drawback to receiving, is the failure to ask, believing. Believing is the key! Here, the bottom line to embrace is this: YeHoVaH has already given His consent:

2 Corinthians 1:20

20 For all the promises of God in him are yea, and in him Amen, unto the glory of God by us.

All promises of YeHoVaH in Yeshua are yes, it is yours! They are "Amen"[65]. In other words, when you ask YeHoVaH to bring to pass any of His promises, including provisionally (spiritual, emotional, mental or physical), He simply says, "Yes, as you have said it".

This goes along with a certain principle in the book of Numbers. While this principle, as seen here, responds to grumbling and complaining, it is a principle that shows us how YeHoVaH responds to our words:

Numbers 14:28

"Say unto them, [As truly as] I live, saith YeHoVaH, as ye have spoken in mine ears, so will I do to you:"

YeHoVaH brings forth in your life, as your words decree. Yeshua said basically the same thing:

---

[65] As I write this book, it is noted that some believers, today, do not say Amen. They've been told that "Amen" is the name of an Egyptian god. Amen, is an original Hebrew word. It means, firmly agreeing with what's been said. Should you want more information on this word, try googling it. One interesting sight is "The Hebrew root of Amen by 119 Ministries". [Please note, this is not an endorsement for this site. It is simply a site to check out the Hebrew root word.]

Mark 11:23

> For verily I say unto you, That whosoever shall say unto this mountain, Be thou removed, and be thou cast into the sea; and shall not doubt in his heart, but shall believe that those things which he saith shall come to pass; *he shall have whatsoever he saith.*

Along these same lines, Yeshua is recorded as saying:

John 14:13-14

> 13 And whatsoever ye shall ask in my name, that will I do, that the Father may be glorified in the Son. 14 If ye shall ask any thing in my name, I will do it.

John 16:23-24

> 23 ¶ And in that day ye shall ask me nothing. Verily, verily, I say unto you, Whatsoever ye shall ask the Father in my name, he will give it you. 24 Hitherto have ye asked nothing in my name: ask, and ye shall receive, that your joy may be full.

Mark 11:24

> 24 Therefore I say unto you, What things soever ye desire, when ye pray, believe that ye receive [them], and ye shall have [them].

This aspect of the kingdom, Yeshua spoke about in a parable found in Matthew 13:33:

> 33 Another parable spake he unto them; The kingdom of heaven is like unto leaven, which a woman took, and hid in three measures of meal, till the whole was leavened.

Leaven, which is yeast, is an active ingredient to make bread rise. Without yeast, certain types of bread are weighty, more like lead than bread. Adding yeast to the formula changes the result, as the yeast slowly works its way into all the ingredients. Once kneaded, it is left alone in a warm place to rise. As time goes by, the yeast does it work, moving through every aspect of the dough, the bread rises and is ready for the oven.

Likewise, the kingdom of YeHoVaH begins small. This is where the new believer grabs hold of heaven and its promises. As the believer moves through their life's struggles, they bring their faith with them, moving from one step to another. In time, their faith effects everything! It effects their life, the lives of their family and friends. It affects even their enemies as they move forward and declare the Word of YeHoVaH. As they move forward in faith, speaking the things of the kingdom of YeHoVaH, and believing YeHoVaH is with them, their faith touches all around them, in one way or another.

In summary, heaven's provisional code is simple:

- You are seated in Messiah in Heavenly places
- From that place, you have all blessings. All blessings include all you need
- You have, therefore, what you say!

What you receive *from heaven* is a good and perfect gift!

James 1:17

> 17 Every good gift and every perfect gift is from above, and cometh down from the Father of lights, with whom is no variableness, neither shadow of turning.

YeHoVaH, the Father of Lights, sends to earth every good and perfect gift, including the "bread" He sent from Heaven, both the bread in the wilderness[66], as well as the Son of YeHoVaH, Yeshua[67]:

John 6:33

> 33 For the bread of God is he which cometh down from heaven, and giveth life unto the world

John 6:48-51

> 48 I am that bread of life. 49 Your fathers did eat manna in the wilderness, and are dead. 50 This is the bread which cometh down from heaven, that a man may eat thereof, and not die. 51 I am the living bread which came down from heaven: if any man eat of this bread, he shall live for ever: and the bread that I will give is my flesh, which I will give for the life of the world.

This powerful aspect of heaven and its principles we see in an item placed within the

---

[66] Which typified Yeshua
[67] Who is the Manna from heaven?

Holy Place. Every item, including this one, helps us to gain a good understanding of what YeHoVaH expects His priests to know and experience. As one enters the Holy Place, there sits a golden table, upon which sits loaves of bread. It is called the Table of Shewbread. Among the many things this table represents, a detailed study of this table shows it typifies Yeshua! He is our bread of life!

Get the picture here!

Yeshua is our bread of life. He came down from heaven, bringing with Him an everlasting covenant. Those who partake of that covenant, partake of Him:

John 6:54-58

> 54 Whoso eateth my flesh, and drinketh my blood, hath eternal life; and I will raise him up at the last day. 55 For my flesh is meat indeed, and my blood is drink indeed. 56 He that eateth my flesh, and drinketh my blood, dwelleth in me, and I in him. 57 As the living Father hath sent me, and I live by the Father: so he that eateth me, even he shall live by me. 58 This is that bread which came down from

heaven: not as your fathers did eat manna, and are dead: he that eateth of this bread shall live for ever.

We partake of Him, as we enter that covenant that He made for us and with us. From our position within that covenant we sit with Him! Due to our position in Him, all we need is secured and already waiting for us.

Just as Yeshua came down to earth, that "bread of heaven", so does every answer to prayer, no matter the depth of that need. It comes, released immediately. It may seem like it delays, but rather than meditate on its delay, praise YeHoVaH that it's on its way! Receive it by faith, first. Let your words echo that of YeHoVaH's and be "yes and amen!" (meaning, I firmly agree with what's being said, e.g. YeHoVaH's promises).

As we continue our study on heaven, as we look at the various aspects of heaven, let's remember how thoroughly we're connected with heaven! Let's remember that Yeshua spent a fair amount of time speaking on the kingdom of heaven to show us that exact thing. He did so that we'd understand how heaven works upon the earth! As Yeshua came down from heaven, all we need comes down from heaven in His Name. Heaven and its principles are seen in the life of Yeshua, work through Him, and through those who live in Him, as the principles are the same.

So, what is heaven's provisional code established by Heaven's Perfect Provider? It is YeHoVaH's answer to your every claim to His promises, which includes your daily bread.

**Heaven's Provisional code
established by Heaven's Perfect Provider
is a simple
YES & AMEN**

PERSONAL REFLECTION:

Think about these aspects of the kingdom of YeHoVaH. Ask YeHoVaH if you understand your place in the heavenlies, and if so, do you operate from that place. Then discuss this question with YeHoVaH, "Is it right to reach into Your kingdom by faith and receive what I need!"

HEAVEN'S WATCHFUL EYE

Because David did that which was right in the eyes of YeHoVaH and turned not aside from any thing that he commanded him all the days of his life, save only in the matter of Uriah the Hittite.

1 Kings 15:5

Today, we have a well-known expression, namely, "the way I see it." From online news commentaries to music on the hit parade, this popular phrase makes a statement, expressing an individual's viewpoint. While some of these viewpoints are often humourous or interesting to hear, scripture, frowns on taking such viewpoints as gospel truth.

In the eyes of scripture, when it comes to God's perception of an individual's rights, or their overall character, He has certain guidelines. "The way we see it", just won't cut it, unless our viewpoint matches His. Believers learn early in their Christian walk to embrace the Word of God, renew their mind, learning to perceive things the same way as YeHoVaH.

In the art of getting along with another individual, it is best when two people meet, communicate with each other, affirm one another, and are like-minded. This helps them to walk in the same direction.

Amos 3:3

> 3 Can two walk together, except they be agreed?[68]

For someone to walk with God, first, they must *meet* God. Then, if they wish *to walk* with God, they need to be *like-minded*. It is imperative to our relationship with YeHoVaH for us to learn to perceive things in the same manner as He perceives them. When we do, assuredly we find comments from the Almighty showing His

---

[68] The Hebrew meaning, when translated a little clearer, states two must meet each other, before they can walk together.

pleasure, words like those spoken of the saints of old:

1 Kings 15:11

> 11 And Asa did that which was right in the eyes of YeHoVaH, as did David his father.

1 Kings 22:43 a

> 43 a And he walked in all the ways of Asa his father; he turned not aside from it, doing that which was right in the eyes of YeHoVaH:

2 Chronicles 14:2

> 2 And Asa did that which was good and right in the eyes of YeHoVaH his God:

In these passages, we hear of those who aligned their ways with the desires of YeHoVaH, walking like their Father who did right. They did not turn away, but rather walked in a manner which was right in the eyes of YeHoVaH.

Not all the kings of Israel, however, received such a glowing accolade:

1 Kings 16:25

25 But Omri wrought evil in the eyes of YeHoVaH, and did worse than all that were before him.

Examples from the scriptures shows us that what God calls good, we should call good. What God calls evil; we should call evil. When we do that, we see "eye to eye" with YeHoVaH, and thus, please Him. He is very displeased when the opposite occurs, as can be seen in the following passage:

Isaiah 5:18-24

> 18 Woe unto them that draw iniquity with cords of vanity, and sin as it were with a cart rope: 19 That say, Let him make speed, [and] hasten his work, that we may see [it]: and let the counsel of the Holy One of Israel draw nigh and come, that we may know [it]! 20 Woe unto them that call evil good, and good evil; that put darkness for light, and light for darkness; that put bitter for sweet, and sweet for bitter! 21 Woe unto [them that are] wise in their own eyes, and prudent in their own sight! 22 Woe unto [them that are] mighty to drink wine, and

men of strength to mingle strong drink: 23 Which justify the wicked for reward, and take away the righteousness of the righteous from him! 24 Therefore as the fire devoureth the stubble, and the flame consumeth the chaff, [so] their root shall be as rottenness, and their blossom shall go up as dust: because they have cast away the law of YeHoVaH of hosts, and despised the word of the Holy One of Israel.

Scripturally speaking, the word "woe" means sorrow or trouble, therefore, great troubles come to those who do not see eye to eye with the Almighty. Regarding heaven, life here is really, all about heaven! The sooner we learn that lesson, and then learn to agree with the viewpoint of the Almighty, the sooner we align with His will and walk in His ways, the better.

While all this is extremely important and imperative to our behaviour, there are additional aspects to the words "eyes of YeHoVaH". We see that in the following scripture:

2 Chronicles 16:7-9a

> 7 ¶ And at that time Hanani the seer came to Asa king of Judah, and said unto him,

Because thou hast relied on the king of Syria, and not relied on the LORD thy God, therefore is the host of the king of Syria escaped out of thine hand. 8 Were not the Ethiopians and the Lubims a huge host, with very many chariots and horsemen? yet, because thou didst rely on the LORD, he delivered them into thine hand. 9 For the eyes of the LORD run to and fro throughout the whole earth, to shew himself strong in the behalf of them whose heart is perfect toward him. Herein thou hast done foolishly: therefore from henceforth thou shalt have wars.

As YeHoVaH carefully watches over the earth, looking upon its inhabitants, He loves to find places where His Help is desired, appreciated, and will show Him to others as the Almighty One. In that way, more people can come to know Him. More people can embrace His ways, and more people will embrace and receive eternal life.

Believers don't necessarily see YeHoVaH as looking over the earth. They do not perceive Him as interested in every aspect of their life. Those who believe that are mistaken! YeHoVaH watches over the entire earth, especially watching over the lives of those who claim to know Him.

In the previous scriptural example, (2 Chronicles 16:7-9), a King of Judah faced an enemy attack. Rather than trust in the Almighty, the king invited the Assyrians to be his strong front. This place in history, a scene for a battle, provided opportunity to see the mighty hand of the Almighty move on behalf of Judah, yet Judah's king was short-sighted. He did not call upon YeHoVaH, and consequently, lost the opportunity to glorify the name of YeHoVaH. He also incurred YeHoVaH's displeasure.

Here is a good lesson for us! When we have troubles, even some which we might, inadvertently, invite, we still have an awesome God to Whom we may call to see our deliverance, but more importantly, to see the name of YeHoVaH glorified. Scripture would have us learn to glorify His Name:

Psalm 96:8

> Give unto YeHoVaH the glory [due unto] his name: bring an offering, and come into his courts.

In speaking of the courts of the Almighty, reference is made to His Tabernacle. In both the Tabernacle of Moses, as well as in the Temple of Solomon, there stood a very specific item which clearly depicted the eyes of YeHoVaH. That item was the 7-branch Menorah.

Once inside the Tabernacle, there was but one light by which to see, and that was by the continuous glow of the 7 branch Menorah. Daily, without fail, the priest tended to these lights to ensure all seven burned brightly. These lights shone for the priests to see, and they represented the eyes of YeHoVaH.

Later, in the book of Revelation, we see them clearly defined and depicted as the seven Spirits of the Almighty:[69]

Revelation 1:4

> 4 John to the seven churches which are in Asia: Grace be unto you, and peace, from him which is, and which was, and which is

---

[69] There is one Holy Spirit. The number 7 means complete, so these are a representation of the Holy Spirit, which is the Spirit of YeHoVaH, the same Spirit of Yeshua.

to come; and from the seven Spirits which are before his throne;

Revelation 3:1

1 And unto the angel of the church in Sardis write; These things saith he that hath the seven Spirits of God, and the seven stars; I know thy works, that thou hast a name that thou livest, and art dead.

Revelation 4:5

4:5 And out of the throne proceeded lightnings and thunderings and voices: and there were seven lamps of fire burning before the throne, which are the seven Spirits of God. [70]

Revelation 5:6

6 And I beheld, and, lo, in the midst of the throne and of the four beasts, and in the midst of the elders, stood a Lamb as it had been slain, having seven horns and seven eyes, which are the seven Spirits of God sent forth into all the earth.

---

[70]*This we'll look at later*

YeHoVaH has but one Holy Spirit, but it is here depicted to show various aspects of the Holy Spirit. Some of those aspects are as follows:

- YeHoVaH expresses His Pleasure and gives grace to those in need. Certainly, the churches in the book of Revelation, with what they were to experience needed the power of Grace so they could stand in those hard and difficult times. Hebrews 4:16 *"Let us therefore come boldly unto the throne of grace, that we may obtain mercy, and find grace to help in time of need.*

- YeHoVaH sees the works of His people. Nothing hides from the eyes of YeHoVaH. His Spirit sees all! Hebrews 4:13 *"Neither is there any creature that is not manifest in His sight: but all things are naked and opened unto the eyes of Him with Whom we give an account."*

- YeHoVaH's eyes, shown in the Menorah, which represents the seven spirits of God, show us that He sees all things, those before His throne and everywhere else. (Revelation 4:5)[71]

---

[71] Seven lamps of fire burning before the throne, which are the seven Spirits of God.

In this scene, the Apostle John stands to receive a revelation of the future.

- YeHoVaH sees the future. (Isaiah 46:10) "Declaring the end from the beginning, and from ancient times [the things] that are not [yet] done, saying, My counsel shall stand, and I will do all my pleasure:"
- YeHoVaH displays His Spirit within the presentation to the Apostle, John, of Yeshua as the Lamb of God. Here, scripture relates to us that the seven Spirits of Elohim are sent forth into all the earth. YeHoVaH has a far-reaching extent to His sight, and nothing hinders it! "The eyes of YeHoVaH [are] in every place, beholding the evil and the good." (Proverbs 15:3)

There are many more aspects of the Holy Spirit of the Almighty, but a look at these few show us that YeHoVaH sees into every aspect of the earth, into every life, and beyond that. His sight is pure, exacting, with no prejudice or slanted viewpoint. He judges fairly and responds wisely, even in situations where evil pokes its head, YeHoVaH has a response, tempered, of course, with mercy.

Psalm 7:11-13

> 11 God judgeth the righteous, and God is angry [with the wicked] every day. 12 If he turn not, he will whet his sword; he hath bent his bow, and made it ready. 13 He hath also prepared for him the instruments of death; he ordaineth his arrows against the persecutors.

Yeshua, upon the earth, walked in the full power of the Holy Spirit.

Isaiah 11:2-4

> 2 And the spirit of YeHoVaH shall rest upon him, the spirit of wisdom and understanding, the spirit of counsel and might, the spirit of knowledge and of the fear of YeHoVaH; 3 And shall make him of quick understanding in the fear of YeHoVaH: and he shall not judge after the sight of his eyes, neither reprove after the hearing of his ears: 4 But with righteousness shall he judge the poor, and reprove with equity for the meek of the earth: and he shall smite the earth with the rod of his mouth, and with the breath of his lips shall he slay the wicked.

Here we see 7 qualities or aspects of the Spirit which rested upon Yeshua. Six are found in verse 2, and the seventh in verse 4:

1. Wisdom
2. Understanding
3. Counsel
4. Might
5. Knowledge
6. Fear of YeHoVaH
7. Righteous Judgment

In heaven's viewpoint, the eyes of YeHoVaH burn bright, without any impairment. He has no vision problems. He sees all clearly! Yeshua's life manifested that pure sight. The Word of God, (Yeshua and the written Word) constantly show the clear vision of YeHoVaH throughout the pages of both the Hebraic and the Apostolic scriptures. He sees all. He judges as He sees, perfectly, without impairment.

PERSONAL REFLECTION

As we look at the seven spirits of YeHoVaH, typified as the Menorah in the Tabernacle of Moses, we see one more attribute. The flames of fire shine brightly within the Tabernacle in Heaven. Yeshua is also depicted as having "eyes as a flame of fire".

Revelation 1:14

> His head and his hairs were white like wool, as white as snow; and his eyes were as a flame of fire;

Do you think of Yeshua in this fashion? Do you see YeHoVaH, looking with penetrating eyes into your life to watch over you, to help you and assist you? Do you see Him as standing close by and responding as you need Him to do? Do you make room in your life to glorify His name?

Why not take some time, before moving on to the next chapter, and speak to YeHoVaH about the wonderful care He gives to you, as He looks over your life as Heaven's Watchful Eye?

HEAVEN'S POWERFUL INCENSE

"Behold, I build an house to the name of YeHoVaH my God, to dedicate it to him, and to burn before him sweet incense, and for the continual shewbread, and for the burnt offerings morning and evening, on the sabbaths, and on the new moons, and on the solemn feasts of YeHoVaH our God. This is an ordinance for ever to Israel."

2 Chronicles 2:4

King Solomon, the royal son and heir to the throne of his father David, built and dedicated a temple to the name of YeHoVaH. Part of that dedication included the burning of sweet incense, which, in accordance with the instructions in the Torah, the Levitical priests presented before YeHoVaH. [72] Solomon knew the importance of presenting things

---

[72] Numbers 16:39-40

properly before YeHoVaH. He knew the consequences of not following the strict instructions in the Torah regarding matters pertaining to God's articles, as given by Moses, for displaying heaven. Such consequences arose earlier, in the reign of King David, his father, when a man, named Uzzah, died, violating an important law of YeHoVaH:

2 Samuel 6:3-8

> "3 And they set the ark of God upon a new cart, and brought it out of the house of Abinadab that [was] in Gibeah: and Uzzah and Ahio, the sons of Abinadab, drave the new cart. 4 And they brought it out of the house of Abinadab which [was] at Gibeah, accompanying the ark of God: and Ahio went before the ark. 5 And David and all the house of Israel played before YeHoVaH on all manner of [instruments made of] fir wood, even on harps, and on psalteries, and on timbrels, and on cornets, and on cymbals."

> "6 ¶ And when they came to Nachon's threshingfloor, Uzzah put forth [his hand] to the ark of God, and took hold of it; for the oxen shook [it]. 7 And the anger of YeHoVaH was kindled against Uzzah; and

God smote him there for [his] error; and there he died by the ark of God. 8 And David was displeased, because YeHoVaH had made a breach upon Uzzah: and he called the name of the place Perezuzzah to this day."

Every article within the Tabernacle of Moses spoke about heaven, as did the identical articles in the Temple of Solomon. God's specific instructions for making, positioning and moving each article, *if disobeyed* meant disastrous results. This was the way it was since God wanted the picture of heaven to be kept perfect and intact. In that way, man would see the pattern and understand it. Violate or alter that pattern and you distort the message!

THE USE OF INCENSE

While incense, to the mind of a reader, might seem like a small, insignificant thing, it was not! Incense, presented in God's way, timing and fashion, represented something very powerful in heaven, and thus, its very essence, including its use was specifically detailed when given by YeHoVaH. Many violated that prescribed order, unfortunately.

One example we find in the book of Leviticus and another in the book of 2 Chronicles.

Leviticus 10:1-3

> 1 And Nadab and Abihu, the sons of Aaron, took either of them his censer, and put fire therein, and put incense thereon, and offered strange fire before YeHoVaH, which he commanded them not. 2 And there went out fire from YeHoVaH, and devoured them, and they died before YeHoVaH. 3 Then Moses said unto Aaron, This is it that YeHoVaH spake, saying, I will be sanctified in them that come nigh me, and before all the people I will be glorified. And Aaron held his peace.

In this passage of scripture, we see two sons of Aaron, who came from the appointed tribe to serve in the Tabernacle, violated the specific command of YeHoVaH regarding the exactness of presenting an incense offering. As a result, they both died!

In 2 Chronicles, we hear about a violation of King Uzziah of Judah:

2 Chronicles 26:16-21

16 But when he[73] was strong, his heart was lifted up to [his] destruction: for he transgressed against YeHoVaH his God, and went into the temple of YeHoVaH to burn incense upon the Altar of incense. 17 And Azariah the priest went in after him, and with him fourscore priests of YeHoVaH, [that were] valiant men: 18 And they withstood Uzziah the king, and said unto him, [It appertaineth] not unto thee, Uzziah, to burn incense unto YeHoVaH, but to the priests the sons of Aaron, that are consecrated to burn incense: go out of the sanctuary; for thou hast trespassed; neither [shall it be] for thine honour from YeHoVaH God.

19 Then Uzziah was wroth, and [had] a censer in his hand to burn incense: and while he was wroth with the priests, the leprosy even rose up in his forehead before the priests in the house of YeHoVaH, from beside the incense Altar. 20 And Azariah the chief priest, and all the priests, looked upon him, and, behold, he [was] leprous in

---

[73] King Uzziah

his forehead, and they thrust him out from thence; yea, himself hasted also to go out, because YeHoVaH had smitten him. 21 And Uzziah the king was a leper unto the day of his death, and dwelt in a several house, [being] a leper; for he was cut off from the house of YeHoVaH: and Jotham his son [was] over the king's house, judging the people of the land.

This scripture speaks of Uzziah, Judah's king, when he became proud in his heart. He determined to take upon himself an office not appointed to him and offer incense to YeHoVaH. As he entered the temple to offer the incense, the shocked priests did their best to deter him. Uzziah refused their resistance, counsel and pleading. Nevertheless, he pushed forward, transgressing in this action to offer incense. As a result, leprosy came upon his body. He was never cured but died a leprous man.

- Why did YeHoVaH react so strongly in both situations mentioned above?
- What did incense represent that its presentation might not be changed in any way?

Part of the answer to these questions rests in understanding what incense represents, so let's jump ahead to the book of Revelation, where we see the clear, and very specific representation of incense defined:

Revelation 5:7-8

> 7 And he came and took the book out of the right hand of him that sat upon the throne. 8 And when he had taken the book, the four beasts and four [and] twenty elders fell down before the Lamb, having every one of them harps, and golden vials full of odours (incense) which are the prayers of saints.

As seen in this scripture, we're told that the vials of incense[74] represent the prayers of the saints. In addition, we're told where these vials of incense appear in heaven:

Revelation 8:3-5

> 3 And another angel came and stood at the altar, having a golden censer; and there was given unto him much incense, that he should offer it with the prayers of all saints upon the golden altar which was before the

---

[74] Odours in Strong's is G2368, an aromatic substance burnt, incense

throne. 4 And the smoke of the incense, which came with the prayers of the saints, ascended up before God out of the angel's hand. 5 And the angel took the censer, and filled it with fire of the altar, and cast it into the earth: and there were voices, and thunderings, and lightnings, and an earthquake.

Heaven's original copy, The Tabernacle in Heaven, like its man-made copy on earth, has only one altar where incense arises, and that is the Altar of incense. Here, in accordance with the clear interpretation of scripture from the book of Revelation, YeHoVaH hears and answers prayers. The answers, in part, are seen in verse 5, where the angel took the censer, filled it with fire from the Altar[75] and sent the whole thing back to the earth.

In looking at the fire added to the incense, we must remember, in the Tabernacle of Moses, there was one and only one place where "fire" burned on an altar. That altar was the brazen Altar.[76] A priest retrieved a hot coal from off

---

[75] Brazen altar
[76] No fire burned on the altar of incense. Coals were added to ignite the incense.

that Altar[77] and placed it in the censer to ignite the incense. That typology is amazing, as it speaks further about Yeshua. Remember, Yeshua is the sacrificial Lamb, typified in the Brazen Altar. Coals from that Altar, which saw the perfect sacrifice realized, added to the incense of the saints, brought forth the needed answers. [78]

Yeshua is the perfect sacrifice, which we saw in an earlier chapter. There, we noted that each believer must put their lives upon the brazen Altar, become a living sacrifice, which is their reasonable service. In other words, believers die to their own wants and desires. The depth of their commitment is visible in their behaviour including, in their prayers. Here, upon the Altar of incense, the depth of their commitment echoes in the prayers they offer to YeHoVaH.

Should believers pray and intercede for others, offering YeHoVaH only that which they want and desire, their prayers stink before YeHoVaH! In plain English, they miss it! Followers of Yeshua should offer prayers as He did, with

---

[77] Brazen Altar
[78] We'll investigate this more when we look at Heaven's Great Intercessor and High Priest.

depth and sincerity, within the will of His Father:

Hebrews 5:6-10

> 6 As he saith also in another place, Thou art a priest for ever after the order of Melchisedec. **7 Who in the days of his flesh, when he had offered up prayers and supplications with strong crying and tears unto him that was able to save him from death, and was heard in that he feared**[79]; 8 Though he were a Son, yet learned he obedience by the things which he suffered;9 And being made perfect, he became the author of eternal salvation unto all them that obey him;10 ¶ Called of God an high priest after the order of Melchisedec[80].

Verse 7 speaks clearly of his reverence for YeHoVaH, and what He required, even in His prayer life! We see this reflective in the words, "in that he feared".

---

[79] Bold and italics added for emphasis for this book.
[80] This order of Melchizadec (Melchizadek) is that of Yeshua's priesthood and that of the believers. We'll look at this aspect in the coming chapter.

There's another picture of the Altar of Incense in Heaven, and that is from a scene in the book of Revelation. Here, we see one more thing, which clearly speaks of what God hears.

Revelation 6:9-11

> 9 And when he had opened the fifth seal, I saw *under the altar the souls of them that were slain for the word of God*[81], and for the testimony which they held: 10 And they cried with a loud voice, saying, How long, O Lord, holy and true, dost thou not judge and avenge our blood on them that dwell on the earth? 11 And white robes were given unto every one of them; and it was said unto them, that they should rest yet for a little season, until their fellow servants also and their brethren, that should be killed as they were, should be fulfilled.

This passage refers to a time when the fifth seal is opened. Then, those slain for the Word of YeHoVaH, *(their lives as a testimony to YeHoVaH and His Word)*, cried out to the Almighty One, requesting judgment and retribution for their

---

[81] Bold and italics added here for this book to emphasize the pertinent scripture

death. Here, we also see YeHoVaH's response to what He hears.

Heaven's Altar of Incense is a very eventful and obviously, an effective place. Its lessons to believers are many, including the idea that our prayers, intercessions, and loud crying to YeHoVaH are heard and answered. Its message is also obvious, in that we do it God's way! Let us learn to align our incense before YeHoVaH's Altar of incense with what's on His heart! Let's learn to remember the true and perfect source of our help!

PERSONAL REFLECTION

When you learned to pray or intercede as a believer, did anyone challenge you to ensure you prayed within the will of YeHoVaH? Were you taught to pray in line with scripture, which outlines God's will? If so, are you willing to align your life with the required incense designed by YeHoVaH, namely pray His Way, in His Will, for His honour and glory!

SECTION 4: INSIDE THE HOLY OF HOLIES

THE TORN VEIL:
Intercession's Priest & King
Acknowledge Him
THE FOUR PILLARS:
Access to The Throne
Approach Him
THE ARK:
Heaven's Throne
Worship before it

HEAVEN'S INTERCEDING KING [82]

"Wherefore, holy brethren, partakers of the heavenly calling, consider the Apostle and High Priest of our profession, Christ Jesus; Who was faithful to him that appointed him, as also Moses [was faithful] in all his house."

Hebrews 3:1-2

Last chapter, we discussed the Altar of Incense. In the Tabernacle of Moses, it stood in front of the veil, which blocked the way to the Holy of Holies. Some position the Altar of Incense within the Holy Place, while others place it within the Holy of Holies. The author of the book of Hebrews embraced the latter position.

---

[82] Yeshua is Priest and King, and an intercessor according to the order of Melchizedek.

Hebrews 9:1-4

"1 ¶ Then verily the first [covenant] had also ordinances of divine service, and a worldly sanctuary. 2 For there was a tabernacle made; the first, wherein [was] the candlestick, and the table, and the shewbread; which is called the sanctuary. 3 And after the second veil, the tabernacle which is called the Holiest of all; 4 Which had the golden censer, and the ark of the covenant overlaid round about with gold, wherein [was] the golden pot that had manna, and Aaron's rod that budded, and the tables of the covenant

Wherever the Altar of Incense truly sat, is not the point of this chapter. Rather, our topic is Heaven's Interceding King, Who is none other than Yeshua, in His eternal position as Great High Priest. To understand His role, typified in the Mosaic Tabernacle, we refer to the book of Hebrews. This book tells us much including placement of the articles as well as the required behaviour of the High Priest.

Hebrews 9:5-7

> 5 And over it the cherubims of glory shadowing the mercyseat; of which we cannot now speak particularly. 6 Now when these things were thus ordained, the priests went always into the first tabernacle, accomplishing the service [of God]. 7 But into the second [went] the high priest alone once every year, not without blood, which he offered for himself, and [for] the errors of the people:

Continuing in the book of Hebrews, we're immediately told an important factor regarding Yeshua:

Hebrews 9:8-10

> 8 The Holy Ghost this signifying, that the way into the holiest of all was not yet made manifest, while as the first tabernacle was yet standing: 9 Which was a figure for the time then present, in which were offered both gifts and sacrifices, that could not make him that did the service perfect, as pertaining to the conscience; 10 Which stood only in meats and drinks, and divers washings, and carnal ordinances, imposed on them until the time of reformation.

Hebrews clearly states what the Tabernacle of Moses foreshadowed under the First Covenant, namely, the way in to the Holy of Holies. It was not understood *until* after Yeshua's death, burial and resurrection, when YeHoVaH ushered in the time the author calls, "The Reformation".

| Reformation Greek # 1357 | ιόρθωσις diorthosis dee-or'-tho-sis | Meaning: to thoroughly straighten |

At that time, it became evident to the discerning ear that Yeshua entered Heaven's Tabernacle with His own blood, to obtain eternal redemption for us:

Hebrews 9:11-14

> 11 But Christ being come an high priest of good things to come, by a greater and more perfect tabernacle, not made with hands, that is to say, not of this building; 12 Neither by the blood of goats and calves, but by his own blood he entered in once into the holy place, having obtained eternal redemption for us. 13 For if the blood of

> bulls and of goats, and the ashes of an heifer sprinkling the unclean, sanctifieth to the purifying of the flesh: 14 How much more shall the blood of Christ, who through the eternal Spirit offered himself without spot to God, purge your conscience from dead works to serve the living God?

Now, being sanctified with better things than under the First Covenant (the priesthood covenant at Mt. Sinai), YeHoVaH, through the blood of Yeshua, purges our conscience from dead works to serve the Living God! For this to happen, YeHoVaH appointed Yeshua the mediator of the new[83] *(renewed)* covenant:

Hebrews 9:15

> 15 And for this cause he is the mediator of the new testament, that by means of death, for the redemption of the transgressions that were under the first testament, they which are called might receive the promise of eternal inheritance

---

[83] Many believers call the covenant renewed, since YeHoVaH introduced a holy priesthood at Mt. Sinai, and man desperately failed God. Yeshua completed that covenant giving us a better covenant and better priesthood.

Now, as discussed in an earlier chapter, believers become part of a better priesthood, after the same order as that of Yeshua:

Hebrews 7:11

> 11 If therefore perfection were by the Levitical priesthood, (for under it the people received the law,) what further need was there that another priest should rise after the order of Melchisedec, and not be called after the order of Aaron?

This passage states loud and clear that perfection under the Levitical priesthood did not happen, as it was impossible within that system of worship. Therefore, YeHoVaH inaugurated Yeshua's priesthood *after the order of Melchisedec*, not the order of Aaron.

Hebrews 7:17

> 17 For he testifieth, Thou art a priest for ever after the order of Melchisedec.

While on earth, Yeshua, Who by the flesh came from the tribe of Judah[84], was not part of the

---

[84] Yeshua was born of the virgin Miriam, whose family line descended from that of King David.

Aaronic priesthood. Nevertheless, He was an intercessor, which is the task of a priest. Thus, He bore punishment for the sins of the world. This action of intercession was prophesied in Isaiah:

Isaiah 59:16

> 16 And he saw that there was no man, and wondered that there was no intercessor: therefore, his arm brought salvation unto him; and his righteousness, it sustained him.

Risen by YeHoVaH as an intercessor for all mankind, Yeshua then entered the Holy Places (main tabernacle of Holy Place and Holy of Holies) in heaven itself, and there, on our behalf, He stands before the Presence of the Almighty.

Hebrews 9:24-28

> 24 For Christ is not entered into the holy places made with hands, which are the figures of the true; but into heaven itself, now to appear in the presence of God for us: 25 Nor yet that he should offer himself often, as the high priest entereth into the holy place every year with blood of others; 26 For then must he often have

suffered since the foundation of the world: but now once in the end of the world hath he appeared to put away sin by the sacrifice of himself. 27 And as it is appointed unto men once to die, but after this the judgment: 28 So Christ was once offered to bear the sins of many; and unto them that look for him shall he appear the second time without sin unto salvation.

Having completed all necessary things to reconcile mankind to YeHoVaH, Yeshua now lives to make intercession for all those who draw near unto Him:

Hebrews 7:25-27

> 25 Wherefore he is able also to save them to the uttermost that come unto God by him, seeing he ever liveth to make intercession for them. 26 For such an high priest became us, who is holy, harmless, undefiled, separate from sinners, and made higher than the heavens; 27 Who needeth not daily, as those high priests, to offer up sacrifice, first for his own sins, and then for the people's: for this he did once, when he offered up himself.

With the task of mankind's salvation finished, Yeshua stands as a readied mediator, in all situations whatsoever the believer requires of Him, so that total victory is attained, as believers live their lives to glorify YeHoVaH.

With Yeshua as the mediator of the believer's covenant, and as believers access their priesthood within that covenant, *(the priesthood after the order of Melchizadek),* [85]intercession takes place in the heavenly realms which moves the earth. The only drawback comes when believers fail to utilize their own priesthood or take advantage of the willing and ready mediator standing before the throne of the Almighty. Here is one more reality that points to the fact that heaven is not about tomorrow! Heaven it about today!

Pertinent, now, to the tabernacle in heaven, it is imperative that believers understand, once they are fully immersed by the Holy Spirit (baptized)

---

[85] If you don't understand that priesthood, or if you still believe today's believers in Messiah operate under the Aaronic priesthood, do a study on the matter. If you wish some assistance in that study, "Arising Incense" by Jeanne Metcalf is available as a workbook and study. See the back of the book for publisher contact information to order the books.

into Yeshua, they have access to the heavenly realms today, now as they enter prayer, worship and intercession. Yeshua paved the way into heaven's tabernacle. Thus, His great victory and entrance into the heavenlies makes it no longer necessary to approach YeHoVaH through man's copy of the tabernacle!

Thus, believers who wish to live out their lives before YeHoVaH in Holy Ghost power, learn to operate in their given priesthood. All believers approach YeHoVaH through the torn veil, which depicted the flesh of Yeshua. Through His sacrifice we now have total access to enter the Holy of Holies!

Hebrews 4:14-16

> 14 Seeing then that we have a great high priest, that is passed into the heavens, Jesus the Son of God, let us hold fast our profession. 15 For we have not a high priest which cannot be touched with the feeling of our infirmities; but was in all points tempted like as we are, yet without sin. 16 Let us therefore come boldly unto the throne of grace, that we may obtain

mercy, and find grace to help in time of need.

PERSONAL REFLECTION:
Consider, dear reader, the Great High Priest, Yeshua. Do you draw near to Him? Do you trust Him? Do you yield to His leading and intercede as He desires? Is Yeshua, as Great High Priest, a treasure in your eyes and a worthy One to share your deepest needs, sorrows, or challenges? Think of these things, dear reader, before you read the next chapter.

HEAVEN'S THRONE ROOM[86]

"Justice and judgment are the habitation of thy throne: mercy and truth shall go before thy face."
Psalm 89:14

Thrones, and throne rooms are places of government. God's Throne Room is no exception, as it is a place where decisions are made to run the universe. God's Throne Room, however, houses a very special place that the book of Hebrews calls, the Throne of Grace. In this chapter, we'll look at that throne.

Coming before YeHoVaH's Throne room, as has been studied thus far, requires a careful approach, in which one closely adheres to the specific instructions YeHoVaH laid out in His Word. When properly following procedure, a

---

[86] Yeshua is Priest and King, and an intercessor according to the order of Melchizedek.

warm reception follows. Scripture relates that reception regarding the Throne of Grace:

Hebrews 4:16

> 16 Let us therefore come boldly unto the throne of grace, that we may obtain mercy, and find grace to help in time of need.

These words, "in time of need" show that this approach to the Throne of Grace in heavenly places is for the present time, and it is for those living upon the earth. In other words, believers living upon the earth, now, in this day and hour, may avail themselves of the help given from the Throne of Grace, even though it is within the realm of heaven itself.

This is but one more mention of the believer's access to this aspect of heaven! This is a very important realization:

Those, truly born of the Spirit of YeHoVaH, walk within the realm of heaven, as they live upon the earth.

Believers access the gate to enter. They access the brazen Altar to be that living sacrifice God requires, they accept their priesthood, ministering to both God and man. They sit in Heavenly Places, availing themselves of God's provision, as well as His wisdom and insight. Believers utilize all the benefits of the Menorah, Table of shewbread and Altar of incense, as discussed in other chapters. All access, too, is from their earthly place, within their physical temples, their bodies.

Yeshua's parables make it very clear, regarding this aspect of accessing heaven, now during the believer's existence upon the earth. One parable Yeshua spoke, told of a lord and master of a vineyard and how they treated the owner's servants and son. In another parable, Yeshua spoke about a nobleman from a kingdom, who left it for a time, and then returned. While both parables have similar meaning, in that they refer to rewards for actions on earth, we'll look at the latter parable regarding the nobleman.

Keep in mind this parable of the nobleman, who goes away for a season and later returns, presents deep meaning for those *who live within the kingdom of YeHoVaH*[87] upon this earth. Note carefully the rewards given in accordance with their actions, for likewise, believers who are born of YeHoVaH's Spirit, will give an account

---

[87] Namely, believers in Yeshua

to Him of what they've done with what's been given unto them in Messiah.

Luke 19:11

> 11 And as they heard these things, he added and spake a parable, because he was nigh to Jerusalem, and because they thought that the kingdom of God should immediately appear.

In the opening verse, we have two reasons why Yeshua related this parable to His disciples. In summary, He did so because they had a totally different idea of the kingdom than scripture portrayed.

Luke 19:12-14

> 12 He said therefore, A certain nobleman went into a far country to receive for himself a kingdom, and to return. 13 And he called his ten servants, and delivered them ten pounds, and said unto them, Occupy till I come. 14 But his citizens hated him, and sent a message after him, saying, We will not have this man to reign over us.

As Yeshua relates the comparison to God's kingdom, He shows each servant as given a certain amount of money. Here money typifies what God endows upon believers. There is also a mention of citizens of the kingdom, who did not want this man to reign over them. These are the people of the world who do not like the rulership of Yeshua. They do not value life as God demands, within the confines of God's plan in scripture, thus, they do not bow their knee to Him in words or behaviour.

Then, the nobleman returns:

Luke 19:15-19

> 15 And it came to pass, that when he was returned, having received the kingdom, then he commanded these servants to be called unto him, to whom he had given the money, that he might know how much every man had gained by trading. 16 Then came the first, saying, Lord, thy pound hath gained ten pounds. 17 And he said unto him, Well, thou good servant: because thou hast been faithful in a very little, have thou authority over ten cities. 18 And the second came, saying, Lord, thy pound hath gained five pounds. 19 And

he said likewise to him, Be thou also over five cities.

Each one of these servants, the returning lord found faithful to invest in their master's kingdom. One took his one-pound investment and multiplied it to ten pounds. The other servant took his one-pound investment and multiplied it to five pounds. Delighted in their endeavours to build within his kingdom, the nobleman rewarded them to rule over cities, the first one over ten cities and the second one over five.

This part of the parable teaches us that Yeshua, when He returns, looks to the investment each believer made within His kingdom. Some will reap more than others, nevertheless, each servant of the kingdom Yeshua rewards in accordance with their investment in that kingdom. [88]

Then, the nobleman calls forward a man who refused investment in the kingdom:

---

[88] When Yeshua comes again, believers are rewarded with rulership over kingdoms of the earth. It is good to keep that thought in mind as we weigh out our behaviour before the Living God, daily.

Luke 19:20-23

> 20 And another came, saying, Lord, behold, here is thy pound, which I have kept laid up in a napkin: 21 For I feared thee, because thou art an austere man: thou takest up that thou layedst not down, and reapest that thou didst not sow. 22 And he saith unto him, Out of thine own mouth will I judge thee, thou wicked servant. Thou knewest that I was an austere man, taking up that I laid not down, and reaping that I did not sow: 23 Wherefore then gavest not thou my money into the bank, that at my coming I might have required mine own with usury?

This servant disliked his master, greatly. Giving no value to the kingdom nor expressing any desire to invest in it, he simply kept the nobleman's money in a napkin. In other words, he lived for himself, disregarding the importance of the kingdom to either the master or to others[89].

We then hear of the nobleman's judgment:

---

[89] If he invested the money, as the parable goes, if he cared for others, then he would bring them into the kingdom, hence increase His Master's treasures.

Luke 19:24-27

> 24 And he said unto them that stood by, Take from him the pound, and give it to him that hath ten pounds. 25 (And they said unto him, Lord, he hath ten pounds.) 26 For I say unto you, That unto every one which hath shall be given; and from him that hath not, even that he hath shall be taken away from him. 27 But those mine enemies, which would not that I should reign over them, bring hither, and slay them before me.

As a final judgment upon the servant who refused to invest in the kingdom, we see these powerful words, "But those, mine enemies, which would not that I should reign over them, bring them here, and slay them before me.[90]" In other words, those who despise the things of the kingdom of God, do not receive the rulership of Yeshua over them. Instead, they prefer to do their own thing. Their life, lived their way for the flesh, resulted in their reward which was death.

This parable and its meaning, Yeshua amplified in His Words to those who knew about the

---

[90] From the parable found in Matthew 21:33-34

kingdom of YeHoVaH, but refused to obey its principles, and instead imposed their own rules. To those, who truly hated Him, Yeshua made comments like this:

Matthew 21:42-44

> 42 Jesus saith unto them, Did ye never read in the scriptures, The stone which the builders rejected, the same is become the head of the corner: this is YeHoVaH's doing, and it is marvellous in our eyes? 43 Therefore say I unto you, The kingdom of God shall be taken from you, and given to a nation bringing forth the fruits thereof. 44 And whosoever shall fall on this stone shall be broken: but on whomsoever it shall fall, it will grind him to powder.

Yeshua tells it like it is to these false disciples. He relates, clearly, that the kingdom of God shall be removed from them and given to others who bring forth fruit. In other parables and with other comments, Yeshua reiterated the same results for those who do not follow the laws and commandments of the Almighty, but in its place, set up their own laws, practices and religious ordinances.

With straight to the point parables, such as the ones mentioned above, Yeshua makes it very clear that Heaven's rewards are not dependent upon a sole, one-time prayer. It takes a commitment to follow through with deeds for those who confess that they belong to YeHoVaH. It takes alignment with His Will, and His Ways, to the rewards received in God's kingdom.

In addition, in accordance with the words of Yeshua, there comes a sorting process which determines the rewards of individuals within God's kingdom.[92]

Matthew 24:30-31

> 30 And then shall appear the sign of the Son of man in heaven: and then shall all the tribes of the earth mourn, and they shall see the Son of man coming in the clouds of heaven with power and great glory. 31 And he shall send his angels with a great sound of a trumpet, and they shall gather together his elect from the four winds, from one end of heaven to the other.

---

[92] There are other passages which refer to the sorting process, including Matthew 13:41; Matthew 16:27

It is far better to serve YeHoVaH, standing for Him, amidst the troubles that touch our life, and not living according to the world's standards. Then, as we do so, we trust Yeshua to confess our name before YeHoVaH, as He promised for those who overcame in Sardis:

Revelation 3:4-6

> 4 Thou hast a few names even in Sardis which have not defiled their garments; and they shall walk with me in white: for they are worthy. 5 He that overcometh, the same shall be clothed in white raiment; and I will not blot out his name out of the book of life, but I will confess his name before my Father, and before his angels. 6 He that hath an ear, let him hear what the Spirit saith unto the churches.

YeHoVaH did not intend for us to stand alone, without help. That's why He gave believers access to the Throne room and the Throne of Grace! Believers, after praying the sinner's prayer with a lifetime commitment in mind, who live out that commitment to the best of their ability, are wise to access the very Throne Room of heaven, bowing before the Throne of Grace, now, and as said in an earlier chapter, also avail themselves of the Great High Priest, Who ever lives to make intercession for them.

Yeshua's words teach that Heaven gained, is a matter of living within the parameters and principles of God's kingdom. It is living a life, here upon the earth, rewarded for eternity, as we serve our Living God, doing His will, not ours. All those, born of His Spirit, must, therefore, "die" to self and "live for Him"

John 12:24
> Verily, verily, I say unto you, Except a corn of wheat fall into the ground and die, it abideth alone: but if it die, it bringeth forth much fruit.

Access to the Throne room is an invitation to come boldly to the Throne of Grace for help in time of need. It is God's established place for believers to come to receive from Him so they can overcome in every situation they face. God never intended believers to do it alone! Entering the Throne Room of Heaven means clear access to receive all that one needs to live upon the earth during the days of our lives. No matter their length, no matter their struggle, God makes His Throne of Grace available!

If believers stand in troubled times, as they live their live out upon this earth, even though they receive rewards, scripture makes it very clear, their help comes from YeHoVaH! [93]How can anyone stand in their day to day activities without coming before the Throne of Grace, for help in time of need?

When we pray, we lay before YeHoVaH our prayer requests, as seen at the Altar of Incense. There too, we see the answers returned to the earth! Now, moving towards the Throne Room, we move to a deeper relationship in YeHoVaH. We move into the place where we receive YeHoVaH's help to stand for Him, *in our time of need.*

At the Throne of grace, we receive YeHoVaH's strength to resist sin, strength to overcome, strength to walk in righteousness, when all around you, wickedness thrives. This Throne's access to believers represents receiving strength to stand in situations that otherwise would be impossible. In this chapter on the Throne Room, as we think about living out our life before YeHoVaH, and receiving rewards for our behaviour, it is true wisdom to recognize the

---

[93]Psalm 12

access given to believers to come before the Throne of Grace.

All this means humbly coming before YeHoVaH to seek His Face, to receive His help in all our dealings upon the earth, especially, in the avenue of death to self. It shifts us past any surface need, to show us the deeper need to receive from YeHoVaH, what He's promised to us, in order that we may stand and not fall. Later, as once again, we utilize our priesthood and thus stand in intercession for others, we'll have the ability to do what needs to be done. Having availed ourselves of the Throne of Grace, we'll recognize and declare that to God all the glory belongs! We'll declare with our life's goals, dreams, aspirations and successes that God's grace suffices for us!

2 Corinthians 3:4-6

> 4 And such trust have we through Christ to God-ward: **5 Not that we are sufficient of ourselves to think any thing as of ourselves; but our sufficiency is of God;** 6 ¶ Who also hath made us able ministers of the new testament; not of the letter, but of the spirit: for the letter killeth, but the spirit giveth life.

PERSONAL REFLECTION:

Take some time, dear reader, and meditate on Heaven's Throne room. Think about a throne, its purpose and why God made this very important part of God's Government available to the believer. You might consider asking Him questions such as:

- Do you access the Throne in the way that He designed?
- Do you come before Him with agendas pleasing to Him, or conversely, offensive to Him?
- Do you need to adjust your life in any way so that you delight His heart!

Such reflections draw you nearer to the One Who redeemed you! May YeHoVaH bless you as you take this personal time with Him.

HEAVEN'S PREVAILING PRESENCE

1 *"O come, let us sing unto YeHoVaH: let us make a joyful noise to the rock of our salvation. 2 Let us come before his presence with thanksgiving and make a joyful noise unto him with psalms. 3 For YeHoVaH is a great God, and a great King above all gods."*

Psalm 95:1-3

King David in his many psalms, sang and wrote much about his God, including attributes of His Presence:

Psalm 139:7-13

7 Whither shall I go from thy spirit? or whither shall I flee from thy presence? 8 If I ascend up into heaven, thou art there: if I make my bed in hell, behold, thou art there. 9 If I take the wings of the morning, and dwell in the uttermost parts of the sea; 10

> Even there shall thy hand lead me, and thy right hand shall hold me. 11 If I say, Surely the darkness shall cover me; even the night shall be light about me. 12 Yea, the darkness hideth not from thee; but the night shineth as the day: the darkness and the light are both alike to thee. 13 For thou hast possessed my reins: thou hast covered me in my mother's womb.

Here, we see David's concept of YeHoVaH's prevalent and prevailing presence on the earth. In every part of David's life, no matter where David went, no matter the circumstances, whether dire or pleasant, no matter the height or depth of David's activities during his lifetime, he knew he'd find YeHoVaH's presence.

As David depended entirely upon YeHoVaH to establish his reign, his territory and extent of his throne and power, he knew the presence of YeHoVaH carefully watched over him:

Psalm 1211-4[94]:
> 1 I will lift up mine eyes unto the hills, from whence cometh my help. 2 My help cometh from YeHoVaH, which made heaven and earth. 3 He will not suffer thy foot to be moved: he that keepeth thee will not slumber. 4 Behold, he that keepeth Israel shall neither slumber nor sleep.

Many Psalms, some authored by King David and some not, mention YeHoVaH's presence, with astounding characteristics, for which mankind should pay attention:
- The earth shook at YeHoVaH's presence, when He descended upon Mt. Sinai (Psalm 68:8)
- The hills melted like wax at the presence of YeHoVaH (Psalm 97:5)
- Tremble, thou earth, at the presence of YeHoVaH, at the presence of the God of Jacob (Psalm 114:7)

Truly, the Presence of the Almighty upon this earth is mighty! That being the case, what is

---

[94]Some biblical scholars attribute Psalm 121 to King David, while others attribute it to another. No matter who wrote it, the principle mentioned here is solid, and that is, God watches over His People.

that presence like, where the fullness of YeHoVaH dwells within the limits of heaven and in the very Throne Room? John, the Apostle, privileged by YeHoVaH to see the Throne Room of heaven, writes of his experience:

> Revelation 4:1-2
> 1 After this I looked, and, behold, a door [was] opened in heaven: and the first voice which I heard [was] as it were of a trumpet talking with me; which said, Come up hither, and I will shew thee things which must be hereafter. 2 And immediately I was in the spirit: and, behold, a throne was set in heaven, and [one] sat on the throne.

While the purpose of John's experience was relative to revelation of future events, nevertheless, he saw the throne and the One Who sat upon it, and accurately related it to us:

> Revelation 4:3-4
> 3 And he that sat was to look upon like a jasper and a sardine stone: and [there was] a rainbow round about the throne, in sight like unto an emerald. 4 And round about

the throne [were] four and twenty seats: and upon the seats I saw four and twenty elders sitting, clothed in white raiment; and they had on their heads crowns of gold.

God's magnificence left John struck with awe. In his attempt to describe this majestic scene, he compared the glory he saw to precious gemstones, which in his time, would be treasured possessions. Next, John relates that 24 thrones were around the main throne, and on those thrones sat 24 elders dressed in white and wearing golden crowns. Suddenly, amid this visual heavenly experience, John hears sound:

Revelation 4:5
5 And out of the throne proceeded lightnings and thunderings and voices: and [there were] seven lamps of fire burning before the throne, which are the seven Spirits of God.

John sees repeated lightning and hears cracks of thunder. His ears pick up voices which filled the atmosphere, as the authoritative and majestic voice of the Almighty speaks from His throne. Suddenly, John's eye gaze upon another wonderful sight. He sees the seven

Spirits of God before the throne. This is the real, true, and perfect realization of the copy of which Moses made, demonstrated to us as *the Menorah*!

Revelation 4:6-7
> 6 And before the throne [there was] a sea of glass like unto crystal: and in the midst of the throne, and round about the throne, [were] four beasts full of eyes before and behind.7 And the first beast [was] like a lion, and the second beast like a calf, and the third beast had a face as a man, and the fourth beast [was] like a flying eagle."

John, once again, uses precious gems of the earth to explain this overwhelming view in heaven that lay before the throne. John sees *a sea of glass, like unto crystal.* His vibrant description continues as he describes 4 magnificent creatures,[95] with eyes in front and in back. Each creature had 4 faces, one like a

---

[95] In Isaiah's vision of heaven, recorded in chapter 6, we see similar creatures to what John saw. In that vision, even the posts of the temple moved. It is possible, therefore, that in the tabernacle of Moses, the 4 pillars before the Throne Room may well represent the 4 faced creatures around the throne. Isaiah 6

lion, one like a calf, one like a man's face, and one like a flying eagle.

Revelation 4:8
> 8 And the four beasts had each of them six wings about [him]; and [they were] full of eyes within: and they rest not day and night, saying, Holy, holy, holy, Lord God Almighty, which was, and is, and is to come.

Here again, there is sound in heaven, as John records these creatures with six wings and full of eyes within, crying out "Holy, Holy, Holy". With their cries they plainly identify to Whom they worship: "YeHoVaH, God Almighty.

Next, John records what happens after the declaration of the four beasts:

Revelation 4:9-11
> 9 And when those beasts give glory and honour and thanks to him that sat on the throne, who liveth for ever and ever, 10 The four and twenty elders fall down before him that sat on the throne, and worship him that liveth for ever and ever, and cast their crowns before the throne, saying, 11

> Thou art worthy, O Lord, to receive glory and honour and power: for thou hast created all things, and for thy pleasure they are and were created

Worship in heaven transcends the human mind, yet as John continues to relate his experience, we grasp the adoration of these magnificent creatures! Then, after the four beasts give glory and honour and thanks to the Eternal One Who sits on the Throne, the 24 elders are moved from their thrones. Immediately, they fall prostrate before the throne and worship the Everlasting Elohim. They cast their precious golden crowns before the throne and say, "You are worthy, O YeHoVaH, to receive glory, and honour and power! They continue to acclaim YeHoVaH's attributes, for He created all things. Adding, all things were created and exist for the pleasure of YeHoVaH.

In the chapters following, John receives specific information as to future events on the earth, but soon, in Chapter 5, he witnesses another dynamic revelation of Yeshua.[96] He is shown as the Lamb of God, the only One worthy to open

---

[96] Earlier chapters show John encountering the risen Saviour in His Glory!

and remove the seven seals on heaven's important scroll, Then, the Lamb is worshipped:

Revelation 5:6-10

> 6 And I beheld, and, lo, in the midst of the throne and of the four beasts, and in the midst of the elders, stood a Lamb as it had been slain, having seven horns and seven eyes, which are the seven Spirits of God sent forth into all the earth. 7 And he came and took the book out of the right hand of him that sat upon the throne. 8 And when he had taken the book, the four beasts and four and twenty elders fell down before the Lamb, having every one of them harps, and golden vials full of odours, which are the prayers of saints. 9 And they sung a new song, saying, Thou art worthy to take the book, and to open the seals thereof: for thou wast slain, and hast redeemed us to God by thy blood out of every kindred, and tongue, and people, and nation; 10 And hast made us unto our God kings and priests: and we shall reign on the earth.

Yeshua, honoured and praised for His accomplishments upon the earth, receives the worship due Him. A new song, commending Him for His worldwide work of redemption, is sung to Him. In thankfulness and admiration to Yeshua the voices cry out, "And hast redeemed **us** and made **us** [97]unto our God kings and priests, and we shall reign on the earth".

Next, John relates the voice of angels, abundant[98] in number. These join the latter praises of the beasts and the elders.[99] These did not join the earlier voices, but now they proclaim great accolades:

Revelation 5:12

> 12 Saying with a loud voice, Worthy is the Lamb that was slain to receive power, and riches, and wisdom, and strength, and honour, and glory, and blessing.

Next, other voices join in the praises:

---

[97] This word "us" indicates the singers (24 elders) have been redeemed, and are therefore, humans who lived before, then died and are now living in heaven, since angels cannot be redeemed only mankind.

[98] He numbers them thousand times ten thousand, and thousands of thousands.

[99] Note: The angels do not sing the song of redemption!

Revelation 5:13-14

> 13 And every creature which is in heaven, and on the earth, and under the earth, and such as are in the sea, and all that are in them, heard I saying, Blessing, and honour, and glory, and power, be unto him that sitteth upon the throne, and unto the Lamb for ever and ever. 14 And the four beasts said, Amen. And the four and twenty elders fell down and worshipped him that liveth for ever and ever.

From John's record, we see that all creation, *whether animate and inanimate*, worship YeHoVaH and the Lamb. Then the twenty-four elders fall prostrate and worship the Eternal One, again.

While our minds might struggle to embrace the totality of this amazing scene in heaven, we can recognize some amazing aspects of heaven including ample evidence to the greatness of the Godhead. In these two chapters in Revelation (4 and 5), we see YeHoVaH, our beloved Lamb of God, Yeshua, as well as the Spirit of YeHoVaH.

In addition, we see and hear of four-faced creatures, angels too many to count, and songs of the redeemed praising the Lamb for His shed blood.[100] Heaven, in this scene, is a place where the greatest reverence and respect gushes forth to the Almighty. Those around His throne love Him and willingly give Him honour, praise and glory.

Heaven's atmosphere immediately around the throne is unlike any throne room on the earth! This is an atmosphere of perfect affection and appreciation to the One, Who cared enough to redeem mankind.

As we look at heaven, especially in this last scene, we see the oneness of Yeshua with His Father. We see all of heaven acknowledging that oneness. Their praises echo throughout the atmosphere of heaven, acknowledging what mighty things YeHoVaH has done. This scene, many believers would like to join.

Praise YeHoVaH! We Can! We can join the praising chorus in heaven from here, upon the earth, and sing warm thanks and praises to the One Who created us, to the One Who redeemed us and to the One Who endeavours to keep us, as long as we wish to be kept!

---

[100]Revelation 5:9

CONCLUSION

"But ye are a chosen generation, a royal priesthood, a holy nation, a peculiar people; that ye should shew forth the praises of him who hath called you out of darkness into his marvellous light:"

1 Peter 2:9

With the amazing scene of heaven, from the last chapter, fresh in our mind, let's point out what we did *not* see in heaven. In doing this, we should see the elimination of non-biblical views on heaven, which are held by many people, including some believers.

- **We *did not see*** people lying around on clouds, playing harps. There is no such scene anywhere in the Bible, not in visions of heaven given to any of the

prophets, nor to Moses, who built a copy of Heaven's Tabernacle
- *We did not see* any fat, half naked babies with wings! This means the Bible does not describe any cherubs in heaven. These are a pagan concept and an abomination in the eyes of the Almighty.
- *We did not hear* or see accolades in heaven given to triumphant people such as King David.[101]. We don't hear praises to Mary (Miriam), the mother of Yeshua. There are no praises given for Isaiah the prophet, nor even Joseph, the son of Jacob, who God raised up to save the family during a famine about to plague the known world at that time. [102]
- *We did not hear* of angels discussing what they might do in order to help someone on the earth attain their destiny.
- *We did not hear* of rooms in heaven with great treasures, including missing body

---

[101] Scripture does not tell us exactly who these 24 elders might be. Possibly, they might be earlier, resurrected saints, however, their identity seems unknown. What we do know is they praise YeHoVaH. So should we!
[102] Their praises are sung in the book of Hebrews, not in heaven!

parts for humans, who through faith can receive them.
- *We did not hear* of our loved ones having a family reunion, or of episodes where they watch over family members still on earth.
- *We did not hear* about most things people say go on in heaven!

None of the above things were mentioned in the scenes of heaven in scripture. Scripture tells us certain specifics because these specifics are what God desires that we know. What we do not know, what we do not see, become areas of faith, where we trust Him with all the unknown aspects of this world, and of course, heaven as well.

What we are told, we treasure. These things we think upon! Heaven's description holds facts about YeHoVaH, His Throne Room, as well as other facts. After all, YeHoVaH, and every aspect of His being, make heaven! This, of a certainty, is the desired focal point of the ones longing to be near the Almighty for all eternity! Surely, this is the greatest treasured possession of heaven! All else pales in comparison to YeHoVaH's person. Nevertheless, as creatures of earth, we need some place to begin, some place to put down our footing. Thus, we embraced the Tabernacle of Moses as the picture for heaven, since this is what God gave to us as a prophetic picture.

We've looked at the gate, which shows one way in; the brazen Altar, which shows the call to believers to lay down their life as a living sacrifice, the Laver, which shows developing Yeshua's reflection in our life, and many other aspects as well.

In the concluding chapters we looked at arising incense, displaying to us the all-important fact that prayers constantly arise before the throne. We hear of mighty answers to those prayers, as a censer is filled with a coal from off the brazen Altar. Although we did not study it, if we look quickly at the vision of Isaiah, we'll see where a coal was taken off the brazen Altar, and used to touch the lips of the prophet:

Isaiah 6:5-8

> 5 Then said I, Woe is me! for I am undone; because I am a man of unclean lips, and I dwell in the midst of a people of unclean lips: for mine eyes have seen the King, YeHoVaH of hosts. 6 Then flew one of the seraphims unto me, having a live coal in his

hand, which he had taken with the tongs from off the altar: 7 And he laid it upon my mouth, and said, Lo, this hath touched thy lips; and thine iniquity is taken away, and thy sin purged. 8 Also I heard the voice of YeHoVaH, saying, Whom shall I send, and who will go for us? Then said I, Here am I; send me.

This vision is one more evident use of the brazen Altar, since YeHoVaH cleanses man from their sins through the *fulfilled aspect* of the brazen Altar.[103] Furthermore, it is evidence of God's greatest desire for mankind: *to enjoy redemption!* This theme, repeatedly, runs like a strong, visible cord throughout the scriptures from Genesis to Revelation, and is also included within the many biblical visions of heaven. Unquestionably, as we look over the many passages of scripture regarding heaven, we see that heaven is concerned with **redemption**.

Heaven, therefore, is concerned with the here and now. That concern wraps itself tightly around YeHoVaH's desire for mankind to enjoy redemption and live an eternal life with Him.

---

[103] Remember, the brazen altar prophetically speaks of Yeshua as the sacrifice for sins.

Thus, our thoughts of heaven, even though poked by curiosity, can take a lesson from heaven, itself! *We should be concerned with redemption of our soul and those of others, for that is what occupies heaven!*

IT'S ALL ABOUT HEAVEN:

As we come, now, to the very last pages of this book, together we've seen that throughout scripture, a certain theme runs from Genesis to Revelation. That theme shows us that life here, is "All About Heaven". We've seen heaven is not about tomorrow! Heaven is about today! It's about entering in the kingdom of God (heaven), here, and then living thereafter for the kingdom of God. In doing so, we exercise our priesthood, becoming that chosen generation, that royal priesthood, that holy nation, that treasured people; that show forth the praises of Him Who called us out of darkness into his marvellous light.[104]

Truly, my dear reader, we've discovered as we did this study together, that heaven encompasses our todays, here upon the earth. Scripture places the greater weight of emphasis on the here and now, and upon our choices

---

[104] Based on 1 Peter 2:9

which affect life here, and hereafter. Through the Word we learn that life here is not a steady diet of pondering, visualizing, or focusing on once we leave these fleshly bodies for eternity. Our choices, here, affect us now, as well as in our afterlife. These choices, in fact, determine our future activities in the afterlife.

As we've mentioned and scripture showed, repeatedly, through the parables of Yeshua and other passages in the Word of God, *Heaven, in its Biblical concept, is not about tomorrow.* It's about today! It is about how we live, *now*, and once born of God's Spirit, it is about how we live *for His kingdom!*

It is just as Yeshua said:

Matthew 13:33

> 33 Another parable spake he unto them; The kingdom of heaven is like unto leaven, which a woman took, and hid in three measures of meal, till the whole was leavened.

In this parable we see a very important aspect of the kingdom of God. Before studying this passage, however, remember the words of Yeshua in Luke 17:21:

Luke 17:21

> Neither shall they say, Lo here! or, lo there! for, behold, the kingdom of God is within you.

One receives the kingdom from YeHoVaH, when one receives Yeshua, for the kingdom of God is within[105] [106]. Now comes the part that must become conscious within us, and that is, *how to align our lives with that kingdom after it takes up residence within.* This, in accordance with scripture, is possible as we, the recipient, become a living sacrifice upon God's brazen Altar, meaning, we die to self.

Then, the kingdom from within begins to move throughout every aspect of our being, just like leaven moves throughout every aspect of dough, prepared for bread, effecting every aspect of our lives. As life in this manner goes on, we're changed, like the bread dough is changed from flat and useless, to raised and ready for baking.

To put it another way, our life changes. We leave a life focused on fulfilling our own will,

---

[105] This is but one more indicator that heaven is not about tomorrow but is about today!
[106] Luke 17:21

following a constant pursuit of attaining all things for creature comfort. We embrace a different life, a different will, a higher will, which is that of our Heavenly Father. This becomes our focus. With the kingdom of God now living within, we willingly step aside and allow the Holy Spirit and the desires of His heart to be freely lived out.

As we do that life's focus shifts. Like the dough in the parable of Yeshua, as we allow every aspect of the kingdom to flow into every facet of our life, we arise to a better life, fulfilling a higher calling! We rise through the Holy Spirit's power to be the sons and daughters of the Living God, just as YeHoVaH originally created us to become, prior to the fall.

LET'S DREAM ABOUT HEAVEN
Before finally concluding this book, let's tie some thoughts together about heaven. Let's presume you fall asleep one night and *you* dream about heaven. Using the information that you have gleaned within this book, let's describe what that dream might look like.

THE DREAM:
As the dream opens, you stand outside the true Tabernacle of Heaven, the one which the

Tabernacle of Moses copied. You are now, in your dream, ready to enter heaven. See yourself walking through the beautiful gate, having accessed it through the precious lifeblood of the only begotten Son of YeHoVaH. In these moments, your thoughts might embrace a true rejoicing, with ecstatic praise, to YeHoVaH for His great and mighty salvation, which you accessed, in order to enter heaven.

Walking inside now, you stand before the gleaming Brazen Altar. There, your thoughts race towards your life's events on earth. You quietly reflect upon life as you lived it thus far. These questions come into your mind:

- Were you that living sacrifice as spoken about in Romans 12?
- What was your reasonable service, if not that?
- Did you give your days, nights and all activities therein to the will and service of YeHoVaH?
- Were you dead to selfish desires?
- Did you hold hands with the world?
- Did you seek to live only for the desires and will of YeHoVaH?

- In *your analysis*, did you love God with all your heart, mind, soul and strength?
- Did you love your neighbour as yourself?

As you leave that impressive Altar, you move towards the Laver. Looking into the clear water, as you're about to gaze into the Laver to see your reflection, further questions enter your mind:

- What will I see in this water? Will I see myself, or will I see Yeshua?
- If I see myself, how much like Yeshua have I become?
- Did I allow the Word of YeHoVaH to change me?
- Did I embrace and allow the idea of the character of YeHoVaH to grip me and change me?
- Have I been a good witness to others, and so much so, they saw Yeshua in me?

Next, you take a deep breath and enter through the first veil, into the Holy Place. You move past those glorious and grand pillars standing so stately at the entrance. As you pass by, you think about the government of heaven, considering how you knew it, when walking out your life upon the earth. More questions flood your mind:

- Were you a good ambassador of the kingdom of YeHoVaH, representing well the government of heaven?
- When you went out into the world, did your efforts produce good fruit for your Lord and Master? Did you get caught up in the glory of those deeds, or were you found humble, giving the glory where it belongs?
- As you lived your faith before YeHoVaH, were you open to and then shepherded by the Holy One of Israel, or did you do your own thing?
- At times, when you were positioned as an under-shepherd were the motives of your heart pure and thus, aligned with those of YeHoVaH[107]?
- Did you *teach and obey* the rules and laws of the kingdom of heaven?

---

[107] You might not be a pastor, but this aspect includes every individual, and those in their personal charge, such as children, grandchildren, nieces, nephews, etc.

- When you operated in the power of YeHoVaH, did you do it in complete alignment with the government of heaven? In other words, did you do it God's way, and in His Power for His Honour and His Glory?
- Did you add to or take away from the Word of YeHoVaH, or did you present it as written?

As the dream continues, you walk up to the Table of shewbread, where more questions flood your mind:
- Did you trust YeHoVaH to be your provider in all things?
- Did you make His Word your main stay, your true substance? Did you live for the bread of heaven?
- Did you recognize and lean upon the Word of YeHoVaH rather than the wisdom of man, or did you operate considering more the fear of man than the fear of God?
- When presenting His Word to others, did you modify it to suit the circumstance, or did you risk the disapproval of man by presenting it in its proper context?

Walking now towards the Altar of incense, the questions continue:

- Did you seek to live a life of prayer, seeking YeHoVaH in every aspect of your life?
- Did you offer gifts of praise from your lips, in all circumstances?
- Did you live by faith in obedience or otherwise?
- Did you live your faith to impress someone who might be looking on, or to bless YeHoVaH?
- Did you take up the cause of the needy, both in prayer and intercession? Likewise, did your feet move to answer whatever needs you could, as instructed by YeHoVaH in His Word?
- Did you learn to pray without ceasing?
- Did you seek YeHoVaH for those who watched over your life, physically and spiritually, or for those in government who watched over the various governmental capacities of your nation?
- Did you rely upon the wisdom of YeHoVaH as you prayed? Were you sincere and focused on truth and the will of YeHoVaH as you prayed and interceded for others?

Suddenly, the fire of the Menorah catches your eye. Your walk towards it. As the light streams steadily upon you, you hear these questions:
- Did you open your life to the moving of the Holy Spirit?
- Did you learn to see things the way YeHoVaH sees things?
- Did you grieve the Holy Spirit?
- Did you look at others, rich or poor or in between, with the same perspective as YeHoVaH, or were you prejudiced in your view of others, or did you make judgments which affected your treatment of others, and in doing so, offend both YeHoVaH and others?
- Were your revelations of the scriptures sourced in the true light of scripture, or were they focused on manmade textbooks filled with the wisdom of man, unanointed and unfurnished by YeHoVaH?
- Did you seek YeHoVaH and His help, wisdom and insight in all things, or did you embrace worldly philosophies and teachings of man?
- What spirit motivated and moved your heart?

Next, you are drawn to the Throne Room and the Holy of Holies. A greater sense of YeHoVaH's holiness touches you, more than ever before in your life. As you come closer, you pass by the four pillars, and suddenly, you hear majestic voices singing, "Holy, Holy, Holy is YeHoVaH of Hosts". Looking towards the throne of the Almighty, a brilliant, almost blinding light shines upon you. More questions flood your mind. You ask yourself:

- Did your voice join in the praises to YeHoVaH's holiness, as you expressed your life upon the earth?
- Did you know and consider His holiness in your life, remembering that your body is the temple of the Holy Spirit, carefully, watching to what you exposed the temple of YeHoVaH?
- Did you partake of and enjoy fellowship with the Almighty on a regular basis? On those same lines, did you carry on two-sided conversations with YeHoVaH, listening to that which was on His heart, or did you merely drop off your concerns and move on?

- Did you stand in His counsel chamber before you spoke, preached, taught or gave advise to others?
- Did you avail yourself of His strong love to love others, even those you considered unlovely?

As the dream continues, you become increasingly more aware of the true holiness and character of the Almighty. Before you know it, you are overwhelmed by His Presence and are face down, worshipping the Holy One, Who gave you eternal life.

One more time, you are grateful for the precious blood of Yeshua, and His payment for your sins. Without that payment, your life would end in eternal darkness, but with it, you can enjoy an eternity with the awesome person of YeHoVaH. Suddenly, YeHoVaH's hand reaches out to touch you. You awaken from your slumber.

REFLECTING ON THE DREAM:
As you contemplate this dream, while it might not mirror the dramatic scenes some declare about heaven, it *is closer in content* to what the Bible teaches. It clearly brings to light how our choices today, affect our eternal destiny! In reflection of the true purpose of life, here, upon

the earth, as you make your life's choices, remember:

Heaven is not about tomorrow.
Heaven is about today.

Let's remember a very positive comment of Yeshua's in John 14: 1-4:

> 1 Let not your heart be troubled: ye believe in God, believe also in me. 2 In my Father's house are many mansions: if it were not so, I would have told you. I go to prepare a place for you. 3 And if I go and prepare a place for you, I will come again, and receive you unto myself; that where I am, there ye may be also. 4 ¶ And whither I go ye know, and the way ye know.

If you are in Messiah, if you are born of His Spirit, then, you are part and parcel of Him. He, Who is Holy and Righteous, keeps His Word. In this you can trust! Therefore, as you think about heaven, reflect on Yeshua's promise that where He is, you will be also! As Yeshua said, You know the Way! A believer's crucified life in Yeshua's terms, is like the "corn of wheat" put into the ground that dies. However, that life doesn't end there! That death, that crucified life in every area of our being, allows for life's true seed to germinate and for YeHoVaH's Spirit life to arise from within.

If your choice is faith in Yeshua, to live the crucified life in Him, know that faith will be proved, tested, and tried. However, once the final curtain is drawn, the stage is empty, and YeHoVaH arrives to speak forth His Judgments, know that you'll have a new life to spring forth, to give honour, glory and praise to the Living God, Who redeemed and kept you!

So, the next time your thoughts run towards heaven and its many wonders, remember, YeHoVaH has put it into the hearts of mankind to consider heaven, while yet living upon the earth. Reflect, therefore, upon His Word and the prophetic picture of heaven you've just studied. Let your thoughts race towards solid Biblical truth and God's call to consider your waiting eternal destiny, and the One with Whom you'll spend it.

Bearing in mind *tomorrow's eternity* as within your grasp, *today*, recognize and weigh out *your necessary choices, at this moment in time*. Forget all thoughts of heaven as a place of your future residence *which has no connection to the here and now*. Rather, think about heaven as readily accessible to you, now! Think about life in the Spirit, accessing what is yours in the kingdom of God, in Messiah.

Dwell on what you can do, now, to touch the lives of others, to go about the business of your heavenly Father. Look at how you can effectively operate within the principles of the kingdom of God. Don't forget, and tell others too, that it is only in *this life* that you gain and access heaven!

Remember, dear one, as you've seen constantly throughout this study, *in the end*, in this life, *really*:

IT'S ALL ABOUT HEAVEN!

APPENDIX

A NAME TO HONOUR

YeHoVaH[108]

"So will I make my holy name known in the midst of my people Israel; and I will not let them pollute my holy name any more: and the heathen shall know that I am YeHoVaH, the Holy One in Israel."

Ezekiel 39:7

If, today, someone asked you to tell them the name of your earthly father, without hesitation you would declare it. If, for some reason, you did not know your earthly father, you would also say so, and perhaps give some explanation as to why you don't know his name. So, if today, you are asked to relate the name of your heavenly Father would you do so with ease, or would you draw a blank?

---

[108] Based on information given by Michael Rood, partly from his work entitled, The Chronological Bible, and partly from his numerous YouTube videos. For more information see his website and/or page 28 of the Chronological Bible.

Most of Christendom, today, is totally ignorant as to the name of the Father, as well as the way it is pronounced. As the author of this book on heaven, I'd like to join the ranks of those who wish to relate that name to the world. After all, when we stand before the Father on the day, we give an account for our deeds in this body, it would be a good thing to know Him, His Name and how it is pronounced!

Did you know that the name of the Father appears at least 6,828 times in the Hebrew scriptures? It is there written as four specific Hebrew letters. They are as follows:

י	Pronounced yode, or yod
ה	Pronounced as hey
ו	Pronounced as Vav
ה	Pronounced as hey

For centuries, whenever the Jews come across these 4 letters they simply say, Adonai, or Ha Shem (meaning the name). They refuse to pronounce the name for several reasons, some of which we will look at momentarily. For now, let's look at whether their tradition affected Christianity. That can be easily done by looking at our Bibles to see if the 4-letter name of the Father is clearly presented or substituted. A quick look reveals that in the KJV Bible, as well as in many other popular versions, the 4-letter name is presented to readers as a 4-letter English word, "LORD". [109] Whether intentional or not, Christendom has followed the ancient tradition of the Jews.

THE ANCIENT TRADITION OF THE JEWS
In early second century times[110] Rabbis hid the pronunciation of the holy name of God. They did this by omitting the vowel pointings, which are necessary to make the name pronounceable. Hence, as they carefully wrote the scriptures, their omittance of the vowel pointings made the name unpronounceable. Historians believe there were two reasons why they did this:

> i. According to Josephus, Rome, under the rule of Domitian, 81 to 96 CE, put to death anyone using the name of the Jewish or Christian God.

---

[109] At times, in certain places, some translators wrote the Hebrew name of YeHoVaH as "GOD" rather than "LORD".
[110] Or according to other authorities, much further back in time.

ii. It is also believed, Rabbis borrowed a tradition from pagans, whereby the name of their god was considered too holy to mention, so they called him "Baal" meaning Lord. The Jews adopted this practice and most still practice it today, even some Messianic Jews!

THEIR TRADITION CONTINUES

Bible translators followed their tradition for reasons which are not presently understood. Possibly, it may have occurred because the pronunciation of the name was totally forgotten, or totally hidden by those who knew[111]. Whatever the reason, following this tradition made the readers of Bibles, who are mostly believers, continue in this tradition. The problem here is not just the tradition, but the bottom line of the tradition is this:

*Does that tradition offend
the Heavenly Father?*

If indeed its origin was Baal worship, then we can give a resounding Amen to the fact it offends God. In addition, as we look at scripture, we see the Almighty was not pleased with this, for His Heart is for all to be saved, including the Gentiles. How can they be saved

---

[111] According to some, the Jews secretly knew the name.

if they don't know the name upon which to call? Scripture [112] clearly states that in the end times, His name would be known so that the Gentiles can call upon it and be saved. Obviously, for that to happen, the name of יְהֹוָה must be made known.

AN HISTORIC DISCOVERY

Today, some Hebrew scholars[113] have searched the world over for Hebrew manuscripts. In doing so, they have found many Hebrew documents which contain the full name with vowels and therefore the pronunciation of the name. These scholars may differ slightly in pronunciation, but nevertheless, they are making the name of YeHoVaH known today.

A DELIGHTFUL SIDE NOTE:

In looking at the Hebrew root of the name of the Father, which is pronounced *Ya-Ho Vah'*, and looking at another scripture, we see something amazing about our Saviour. In speaking of the Prophet, the one the Father would send to Him

---

[112] Jeremiah 16:1-21

[113] Nehemiah Gordon was the Hebrew scholar who found the name of the Father, with all vowel pointings, and through his efforts and those of others, that name with vowels pointings has been found in over 2000 manuscripts.

we all must listen and obey, YeHoVaH said that His name would be in the name of the Prophet.

Exodus 23:21 "Beware of him, and obey his voice, provoke him not; for he will not pardon your transgressions[114]: *for my name [is] in him.*"

Our Saviour's name, as given by the angel was "Yehoshua".

י	**Pronounced yode or yod**
ה	**Pronounced hey**
ו	**Pronounced vav**
ש	Pronounced shin
ע	Pronounced ayin

The name of the Father is in the name of the Son! The first three letters of YeHoVaH show it! (Yod, Heh, Vav). Is it so amazing that the name of our Father is in the true name of the One YeHoVaH sent to redeem us!

---

[114] Please keep in mind that Yeshua bore the punishment for your sins. Your sins were not pardoned, they were atoned!

HONOUR THE FATHER'S NAME

Throughout this book, and all subsequent books, as well as all accompanying audios and PowerPoints, it is the author's intention to widely use, proclaim and continually pronounce the name of the Father. Indeed, this breaks with tradition, but thus far as we've shared the news of the Father's name, reception has been excellent.

NAME CHALLENGE:

Since, as of this reading, you are no longer ignorant of your heavenly Father's name, please join the unofficial network of proclaimers of the Father's name and shout it to the house tops.

Romans 10: 12-15

12 ¶ For there is no difference between the Jew and the Greek: for the same Lord over all is rich unto all that call upon him. 13 For whosoever shall call upon the name of YeHoVaH shall be saved. 14 How then shall they call on him in whom they have not believed? and how shall they believe in him of whom they have not heard? and how shall they hear without a preacher? 15 And how shall they preach, except they be sent? as it is written, How beautiful are

the feet of them that preach the gospel of peace and bring glad tidings of good things!

TABERNACLE CHAPTER RECAP

Item	Ch	Yeshua Depicted as	Yeshua is the:
Gate	2	Heaven's Narrow Way	Perfect & only door to heaven,
			(through Whom we have salvation)
Brazen Altar	7	Heaven's Message & Challenge	Perfect sacrifice, example & challenge
			(in Whose likeness we're called)
Laver	8	Heaven's Majestic Reflection	Perfect Image (WORD) of YHVH,
			(in Whom our cleansing comes)

Five Pillars & 1st Veil	10	Heaven's Unshakeable Government	Established Rulership
			(with Whom we sit & rule)
Table of Show-bread	11	Heaven's Perfect Provider	Perfect Provider
			(in Whom we trust for all things)
Seven Branch Menorah	12	Heaven's Watchful Eye	Flawless Source of Wisdom, Power, and Excellence
			(in Whose guidance we seek)
Altar of Incense	13	Heaven's Powerful Incense	Perfect Source of Help & Needed intercession
			(of Whom we seek))

Torn Veil	14	Heavens Great Intercessor & High Priest	Perfect High Priest, Healer & Intercessor,
			(In Whom we call upon)
Four Pillars	15	Heaven's Throne Room Access	Perfect Access to the Throne Room,
			(in Whom we stand before the throne of grace)
Ark of The Covenant	16	Heaven's Prevailing Presence (Oneness With YHVH)	Perfect Relationship with YHVH
			(In Whom we hear & obey)

SALVATION'S MESSAGE

Yeshua, when walking on earth, said this:

> John 3:14-18wor
> 14 And as Moses lifted up the serpent in the wilderness, even so must the Son of man be lifted up: 15 That whosoever believeth in him should not perish but have eternal life. 16 For God so loved the world, that he gave his only begotten Son, that whosoever believeth in him should not perish, but have everlasting life. 17 For God sent not his Son into the world to condemn the world; but that the world through him might be saved. 18 He that believeth on him is not condemned: but he that believeth not is condemned already, because he hath not believed in the name of the only begotten Son of God.

During the time of Moses, the children of Israel, in the wilderness, rebelled against God, at which time poisonous serpents infiltrated the camp, killing many of the people. After seeking YeHoVaH for a solution to the problem, Moses followed God's instructions and made a bronze serpent fashioned and erected it on a pole in sight of the people. Whosoever wanted to live, must acknowledge their rebellion against YeHoVaH, and in doing so, look upon the erected pole and bronze serpent, to YeHoVaH, who gave them life in place of death, then they would live.

Yeshua said, just as Moses erected that bronze serpent in the wilderness, He would be lifted up. This referred to the event, in the future, of Yeshua's crucifixion. During the time when the serpent hung on that pole, whosoever wanted to live and not die from the serpent's bite must acknowledge their rebellion, their sin against YeHoVaH. Likewise, for those who wish to live eternally, they must look upon the cross of the crucified One, to YeHoVaH, who provided life for them. This was an act of love for all humankind, necessary because man is born from Adam, and thus is born with an inherent sin. Secondly, man sins. The consequence of sin is death, and eternal death, wherein man will spend an eternity in darkness, away from YeHoVaH. Unfortunately, there is nothing humanly possible to reverse those consequences. Even if a person had made a genuine decision never to sin again, and for some reason they succeeded, all their good deeds and good living would not erase the penalty of eternal death.

There is only *one way* for Eternal Life to touch a person's life. That is the way Yeshua explained to His listeners:

through the works of God on the cross of Calvary.

Salvation comes by understanding these facts:
1. Yeshua, being the Son of God and the fulfillment of the scriptures, never sinned
2. YeHoVaH, on behalf of every human being on the earth, chose to make Yeshua become as sin, in His Eyes, so that Yeshua might pay the penalty for sin, for all of humanity.
3. Yeshua paid that penalty. He died on the cross and was buried in a tomb.
4. Three days later, He rose again, appearing to His disciples, to show them the reality of His resurrection, to show them God vindicated Him and made Him both Lord and Messiah.
5. Yeshua could not stay in the tomb, because "death" comes to all who sin, but since Yeshua never sinned, therefore, death could not hold Him in the grave.
6. All those who come to Yeshua, to receive Him as their Saviour, receive liberty from sin and from its horrible consequence, eternal death.
7. They enter YeHoVaH's kingdom and receive eternal life, as well as another gift: **The Righteousness of Messiah.** After salvation, when YeHoVaH looks upon a believer in Messiah, He sees Yeshua's perfect life and sees a redeemed believer, set aside for YeHoVaH. Since salvation has taken place

in the believer, the Holy Spirit dwells within them.

8. All it takes to receive salvation from YeHoVaH is receiving His Messiah, fully repenting from sinning against God. [115] YeHoVaH even gives the believer the faith to receive His gift of Salvation!

The Apostle Paul put it this way:

> Ephesians 2:8
> > "For by grace are ye saved through faith; and that not of yourselves: it is the gift of God"

When you pray the following prayer, realize it is written here to get you started in your walk with YeHoVaH. To be truly saved, you make a life's commitment! There is not just a one-time prayer and you're done! From this moment on, seek YeHoVaH for His help in all things, including to follow through with your commitment until the very end!

---

[115] And against man. When a person steals, etc. they sin against both God and man,

SINNER'S PRAYER
& LIFETIME COMMITMENT

Heavenly, Father:

I acknowledge before You, Lord, that I am a sinner. I understand sin's punishment is a life without You, for all eternity. Thank You for sending Yeshua to the earth, as the Messiah. I understand now that He died in my place, to take my punishment for my sins. I believe You raised Yeshua from the dead, and now that I've I accept Him as my personal Saviour, my old life dies, and my new life begins.

I humbly ask You, Lord, to forgive me of my sins, and as of this moment, I receive Yeshua as my Mashiach. I open my heart to receive the works of the cross that You provided for me through Yeshua, and with Your help, I will walk away from my sin, turning my back upon my own will and ways. I will now live my life seeking to obey Your Word and Your will. Help me to live, from this point onward, in a manner pleasing to You.

Amen

*****

If you prayed that prayer, please be sure you tell someone. Remember that a person believes with the heart unto righteousness and confesses with their mouth unto salvation, as spoken about in Romans 10:10.

10 For with the heart man believeth unto righteousness; and with the mouth confession is made unto salvation

One more thing:

Remember, this gospel message comes with power. When you hear it, the kingdom of God draws near to you. When you repent of your sins and receive Salvation, the kingdom of God moves within. You can't see it, feel it or tell it from an outward observing. It is accepted, received and lived out by faith!

Seek out other believers in Messiah and may God bless you richly as you live your live, now, completely for Him!

Other Books by This Author

An Arsenal of Powerful Prayers [116]
Scriptural Prayers to Move Mountains,
Arising Incense
A Believer's Priesthood
Candidate for A Miracle
Wisdom from the miracles of Yeshua
Foundations of Revival
Biblical Evidence for Revival
His Reflection
What God longs to see in His People
Heaven's Greater Government
Behind the Scenes of Earth's Events
In The Name of Yehovah We Set Up Our Banners
Biblical use of banners
It's All About Heaven
As Pictured in Scripture
Kingdom Keys for Kingdom Kids
Walking in Kingdom Power
Molded for the Miraculous
Why God made You
Releasing the Impossible
The Limitless Power of Intercession
Volume 1: Intercessions from the Author's life
Volume 2: Intercessions from Bibical Characters

---

[116] *This is a book of written prayers of various topics to help believers live a stronger, active faith. No workbook.*

Salvation Depicted in a Meal [117]
Passover Hagaddah
The Jeremiah Generation
God's Response to Injustice
The Warrior Bride-
God's Kingdom Advancing through Spiritual Warfare
Thy Kingdom Come
Entering God's Rest in Prayer
Watching, Waiting & Warning
Obeying Yeshua's Command to Watch & Pray
When Nations Rumble
A Study of the Book of Amos
Worship in Spirit and In Truth [118]
The Tabernacle of David - Past, Present & Future

---

[117] *Haggadah (Guide) for a Christian Passover. No Workbook.*
[118] *Good sister book to "In the Name of YeHoVaH we set up our banners".*

ABOUT THE KING JAMES VERSION

Scriptures quoted in this book *originate* from the KJV **public domain version** of the Bible, which means, no copyright exists on this version of the scripture. While some find this translation outdated, Jeanne, trained in the KJV still finds this version helpful, and uses it in all her books[119].

In using KJV, however, it is good to remember the following:

- Some words in the KJV have changed meaning over the centuries. To understand such words, look up the root word in its original language. In doing so, the meaning stands out. For example. KJV uses the word "conversation" however, in its original language it means moral character, or behaviour.
- When KJV spoke of humanity, they said, "man". When you read that word, or hear others speak about the scriptures using the term, "man", know it refers to all humankind, not a specific gender.

---

[119] In later manuscripts, the author updated the more archaic words in the KJV such as wouldest or couldest.

Due to tradition, the name of the Father, YeHoVaH appears as LORD, or at times as Jehovah. However, in all Jeanne's manuscripts, YeHoVaH's name replaces the term LORD. To learn more read "A Name to Honour", located in the Appendix section.

SCRIPTURE INDEX

1

1 Kings 15:11......... 167
1 Kings 15:5........... 165
1 Kings 16:25......... 168
1 Kings 22:43 a...... 167
1 Peter 2:................ 238
1 Peter 2:9.............. 233
1 Peter 3:22,........... 146
1 Timothy 2:4......... 96

2

2 Chronicles 14:2.. 167
2 Chronicles 16:7-9
.... 171
2 Chronicles 16:7-9a
.... 169
2 Chronicles 2:4.... 179
2 Chronicles 26:16-21
.... 183
2 Corinthians 1:20 156
2 Corinthians 3:4-6218
2 Corinthians 5:10.. 68
2 Corinthians 5:17.. 76
2 Samuel 6:3-8...... 180

A

Amos 3:3............... 166

D

Daniel 4:17;25....... 141

E

Ephesians 1:19-23. 152
Ephesians 1:3........ 151
Ephesians 2:18-22. 155
Ephesians 2:4-10... 114
Ephesians 2:4-7.... 147, 153
Ephesians 2:6........ 154

Ephesians 2:8 268
Ephesians 2:8-10 ... 155
Ephesians 5:25c-26109
Exodus 19: 7-8 128
Exodus 19:16-20 ... 129
Exodus 19:4-8 126
Exodus 19:5 ... 125, 134
Exodus 19:9-13 128
Exodus 20:1-17 130
Exodus 20:19 130
Exodus 23:21 259
Exodus 24:3 130
Exodus 24:7-8 131
Exodus 25:8-9 17
Ezekiel 39:7 254

G

Genesis 37:7 89
Genesis 50:20 89

H

Hebrews 10:7 145
Hebrews 12:2 ... 83, 84, 85
Hebrews 3:1-2 193
Hebrews 4:13 174
Hebrews 4:14-16 ... 202
Hebrews 4:16 174, 206
Hebrews 5:6-10 188
Hebrews 7:11 198
Hebrews 7:17 198

Hebrews 7:25 85
Hebrews 7:25-27 ... 200
Hebrews 8:1-2 145
Hebrews 8:5b 15
Hebrews 9:11-14 ... 196
Hebrews 9:14 86
Hebrews 9:1-4 194
Hebrews 9:15 197
Hebrews 9:24-28 ... 199
Hebrews 9:27 67
Hebrews 9:5-7 195
Hebrews 9:8-10 195

I

Isaiah 11:2-4 176
Isaiah 30:21 40
Isaiah 33:5-6 57
Isaiah 46:10 175
Isaiah 5:18-24 168
Isaiah 59:16 199
Isaiah 6 226
Isaiah 6:5-8 236
Isaiah 7:14 133

J

James 1:17 .... 10, 160
James 1:22-24 110
Jeremiah 16:1-21 ... 258
Jeremiah 17:9-10 68
Jeremiah 6:16 40
John 1:1-4, 14 111

John 10:14 122
John 10:1-5 122
John 10:7 22
John 12:24 .... 36, 216
John 14: 1-4 250
John 14:13-14 158
John 14:6 ...... 22, 31, 42
John 14:9-11 111
John 16:23-24 158
John 17:11-26 112
John 3:14-18 265
John 3:16 19
John 3:2b 73, 74
John 3:3-8 73
John 3:5 78
John 3:6 .... 75, 79
John 3:7 79
John 3:7- 75
John 6:33 161
John 6:38 97
John 6:48-51 161
John 6:54-58 162

L

Leviticus 10:1-3 182
Luke 10:8-11 98
Luke 12:20 67
Luke 17:21 240
Luke 19:11 208
Luke 19:12-14 208
Luke 19:15-19 209
Luke 19:20-23 211
Luke 19:24-27 212
Luke 22:41-44 ... 84, 85
Luke 22:69 146
Luke 23:26-31 51

M

Malachi 2:4-7 100
Mark 10:13-16 104
Mark 11:23 158
Mark 11:24 159
Mark 12:36 146
Mark 16:19 146
Mark 17:21 38
Mark 7:20-23 39
Matthew 10:7-8 99
Matthew 11:28-30 ... 41
Matthew 12:28 97
Matthew 13:11-17. 117
Matthew 13:18-23. 118
Matthew 13:33 ..... 159, 239
Matthew 13:3-9 116
Matthew 13:41 214
Matthew 13:44 .. 45, 46
Matthew 13:45 -46.. 47
Matthew 15:19, ... 38
Matthew 16:24-25... 35
Matthew 16:27 214
Matthew 18:3-4 105
Matthew 21:33-34. 212

Matthew 21:42-44. 213
Matthew 22:13 29
Matthew 23:13-15. 102
Matthew 23:2-4 103
Matthew 24:19-22 ... 53
Matthew 24:30-31. 214
Matthew 25. 90
Matthew 25:14-30 ... 91
Matthew 5:10 55
Matthew 5:20 ... 72, 95, 102
Matthew 6:19-21 60
Matthew 6:21 .... 50, 66
Matthew 6:33 149
Matthew 6:9 5
Matthew 7:14 ... 34, 43, 51
Matthew 7:15-20 ... 105
Matthew 7:21 72

N

Numbers 14:28 157
Numbers 16:39-40 179

P

Philippians 2:12 100
Philippians 2:5-9 62
Proverbs 15:16 64
Proverbs 15:3) 175
Proverbs 16:17 71
Proverbs 22:1 61

Proverbs 3:13-18 63
Proverbs 4:20-27 38
Psalm 103:19-21 139
Psalm 111:10 64
Psalm 114:7 223
Psalm 116:15 9
Psalm 119:89 147
Psalm 12 217
Psalm 121:1-4 223
Psalm 139:7-13 221
Psalm 68:8 223
Psalm 7:11-13 176
Psalm 89:14 205
Psalm 95:1-3 221
Psalm 96:8 171
Psalm 97:5 223

R

Revelation 1:14 178
Revelation 1:4 172
Revelation 21:21 59
Revelation 3:1 173
Revelation 3:4-6 215
Revelation 4:1-2 224
Revelation 4:3-4 224
Revelation 4:5 ...... 173, 174, 225
Revelation 4:6-7 226
Revelation 4:8 227
Revelation 4:9-11 .. 227
Revelation 5:12 230

Revelation 5:13-14 231
Revelation 5:6 173
Revelation 5:6-10 .. 229
Revelation 5:7-8 185
Revelation 5:9 232
Revelation 6:9-11 .. 189
Revelation 8:3-5 185

Romans 1:20 75
Romans 10: 12-15 . 260
Romans 10:10. 269
Romans 12 242
Romans 12:1 83
Romans 12:1: 87

ABOUT THE AUTHOR

Jeanne Metcalf has served YeHoVaH for over forty years. Presently, she serves in the capacity of an ordained minister, working as the Senior Pastor of a ministry, named *"Forward March!"* Ministries. (FMM) FMM is a part of a global grassroots movement of the Holy Spirit to return Christianity to its New Testament roots. Its primary goals include teaching early church concepts, spreading the gospel, and discipling believers so that all can walk in New Testament power, equipped to turn the world upside down with the impact of the gospel.

Jeanne gained credibility as a gifted teacher, writer, and speaker through her activities with FMM. With her passion for souls, a God-given insight and love for the Word of God, Rev. Jeanne presents sound biblical teachings on both the Hebraic and Apostolic scriptures, with clarity and simplicity, in a refreshing straightforward format. Those who study the Bible with Jeanne, highly recommend her studies.

Transformed lives stand as witnesses as through Rev. Jeanne's leadership, believers stand equipped, steadfast in their faith, prepared to live it out triumphantly.

CONTACT INFORMATION

*For more great books or
to contact Jeanne, go to*
www.cegullahpublishing.ca

www.ingramcontent.com/pod-product-compliance
Lightning Source LLC
Chambersburg PA
CBHW070727160426
43192CB00009B/1340